DRUM

AN AFRICAN ADVENTURE
– AND AFTERWARDS

ANTHONY SAMPSON

HODDER AND STOUGHTON
LONDON SYDNEY AUCKLAND TORONTO

British Library Cataloguing in Publication Data
Sampson, Anthony
  Drum.—New ed.
  1. Drum   2. Journalism—South Africa
  I. Title
  079'.68   PN5480.D/

ISBN 0 340 33383 9

Hodder and Stoughton Editorial Office: 47 Bedford Square, London WC1B 3DP.

Drum

This book is to be returned on or before the latest date stamped below.

Also by Anthony Sampson

The Treason Cage
Commonsense About Africa
South Africa: Two Views of Separate Development
The Anatomy of Britain
Anatomy of Britain Today
Macmillan: A Study in Ambiguity
The New Europeans
The New Anatomy of Britain
The Sovereign State
The Seven Sisters
The Arms Bazaar
The Money Lenders
The Changing Anatomy of Britain

For
JIM BAILEY

Contents

Introduction

I began writing my first book *Drum* on my way back from Africa in 1955 on the S.S. *Rhodesia Castle*, a slow boat sailing from Durban to Tilbury via East Africa and the Mediterranean; and I finished it after much hesitancy when I had just started working as a more conventional Fleet Street journalist for the *Observer*. Of my thirteen books it is still my favourite, recording my first intense experience as a journalist, when I was given the rare chance to work closely with courageous and creative people in a community and setting totally cut off from my upbringing. No writer could have hoped for a more challenging beginning: it turned upside-down my political outlook and my view of my own country, as well as of Africa, and influenced all my later interests and books. Compared to the restless curiosities and journeys of later assignments my four years involved with the black townships of Johannesburg gave me the opportunity for a personal and consistent investigation—through a microscope, rather than a telescope—alongside colleagues and friends to whom I owed much.

This book tells a personal and straightforward story, but I like to think that it also throws a few rays of light onto a period of South African history which looks more significant after three decades. It describes a time when the apartheid policies of the Afrikaner Nationalist government—which was then only three years old—were first showing their teeth, and when the black political movements were mobilising for their first serious campaigns, before they were banned, suppressed and driven into exile. The black writers, intellectuals and politicians still had some hopes of being admitted into a wider community, and of sharing power and dignity through peaceful means; and they were much influenced by the American example and by the Western idealism of the post-war years. It was still possible to report black politics without censorship or reprisals, and it was not too dangerous for a white man to spend his time in Soweto, or for black friends to entertain him. To many black writers as well as white visitors it represented a kind of Age of Innocence compared to the harsh repression, the dashed hopes and the mass imprisonments and torture which followed in the sixties and seventies.

The urban black South Africans with whom much of this story is concerned remain, I believe, the most important, and also the least known, element in the future of the Republic. Their attitudes towards the whites, and towards the West, will determine whether South Africa can eventually reach a peaceful solution within the Western community. When I wrote this book white South Africans and the rest of the world took little interest in the sprawling black townships south-west of Johannesburg—Soweto as they later came to be called. In the following decades riots, strikes and police reprisals made Soweto notorious through Europe and America, and white Johannesburgers were compelled to think more seriously about this black city outside the gates. The apartheid policies of the sixties which created the new black Homelands in rural areas assumed that the millions of urban blacks would work in the cities only on sufferance, with no rights or representation. But the problem refused to go away, for the whites needed their labour, their skills and their tacit consent to ensure their economic growth and political stability.

But this is not a book of political analysis or generalisation: it is the story of one young man's adventures with a group of individuals in one African city. In this new edition I have kept the original text unchanged, whatever the embarrassments, but

I have added a long epilogue in which I try to give an account of what happened to the main characters in the story, and to *Drum* itself, in the thirty years since; and to say something of my later experiences of South Africa.

Author's Preface

In this book I have given some account of the odd beginnings of an African magazine in South Africa called *Drum*, of which I was editor for three and a half years. I have tried to show something of the view of South Africa and its problems which I gained from the standpoint of my unusual job, of being white editor of a black paper, and how, in the course of our venture, my knowledge of urban Africans deepened, and I was able to penetrate behind the high wall of apartheid that runs through South African life. I have tried to depict this new, unknown and important Africa of towns and trousers as I discovered it, watching and listening to people, conversations and reactions. I have told the story as plainly as I can, in order not to blur the stark realities of the African situation.

As far as possible, I have excluded myself from the story which is primarily that of the African writers and African readers with whom I worked. I do not wish the inevitable "I" in this narrative to imply that the achievements I describe are my own. The development of *Drum* had its share of mistakes, conflicts, misunderstandings and compromise, with which this story cannot be concerned; inevitably this chronicle is concerned mainly with highlights.

I have refrained from drawing any moral, so that the reader may draw his own. I do not claim to make a detailed analysis of South Africa's immensely complicated problems, which others have already done, and which lie quite outside the scope of this book. I try to show the human situations, the anguish, laughter and day-to-day affairs, which lie behind the South African predicament. I have aimed to convey the important truths of the South African situation in terms of people: for I believe that many of the troubles and conflicts in South Africa, as in other parts of Africa, arise from a basic ignorance of urban Africans and their attitudes; and that it is these people who will, in time, play the decisive part in the future of Africa.

So much of this book is about the doings and writings of others, that my great indebtedness is largely obvious; but I would like to record most of all my thanks to Jim Bailey, who made so much of this story, and allowed me to take the credit; to Henry Nxumalo, Todd Matshikiza and Can Themba for their contributions, comments and suggestions; to all those who played a part in this story whom I have not been able to mention—most of all Peggy Rutherford and Ann Campell; and lastly to Robin Denniston of Collins, for his unwavering confidence and help.

The Frythe, Welwyn
February, 1956

CHAPTER ONE

White Hand

I opened a telegram in London, on Good Friday, 1951:

ARE YOU IMMEDIATELY AVAILABLE JOB NEW NEGRO
PERIODICAL IN CAPE TOWN FIFTY POUNDS MONTH SAY YES
JIM BAILEY

I had first met Jim Bailey two years before, while we were both at Oxford. I sat at the Playhouse one night, next to a man as untidy as I was. We talked. After watching *The Glass Menagerie* for ten minutes he said: "Awful, isn't it? Let's go and have a drink."

Jim was a very untypical undergraduate. He had been a fighter pilot in the Battle of Britain. He owned four thousand sheep and a racehorse stud in South Africa. He combined writing a philosophy thesis on "the history of progress" with buying tractors, thoroughbred stallions and Merino rams.

His father was Sir Abe Bailey, the Johannesburg gold millionaire and racehorse owner; his mother was the first person to fly across Africa. When his father died, Jim took over the family sheep farm and stud in South Africa, and flew back to Oxford whenever he could to write his thesis.

The last time I had seen him, we were drinking at the Angel at Rotherhithe, on a balcony perched over the Thames, watching the flaps of Tower Bridge open and shut, letting ships go down to the sea. We talked about travel and ships and Africa.

"It's all right for you," I said, "you're flying back to Africa tomorrow."

15

"You must come out sometime; you'd like it," he said in his vague way.

And here was the telegram.

My previous career had been neither interesting nor distinguished. After school I had spent two and a half disillusioned years in the post-war Navy, and three idle years at Oxford. I had read 243 Elizabethan plays, written a monograph, "On the Printing of Shakespeare's Plays", and considered myself a high Tory. I left Oxford with a vague desire to do something unusual.

I said, Yes. "But I don't want to get mixed up in politics," I wrote to Jim. I sailed on the *Llangibby Castle* to Cape Town.

Bob Crisp, the editor of *African Drum*, as the magazine was then called, met me at Cape Town. He was a large man in every sense. He was one of South Africa's heroes: he had been a famous Springbok cricketer; a major in the tank corps, with a D.S.O. and bar; a popular journalist and broadcaster. Bob Crisp's new magazine for Africans was big news.

"We're moving *Drum* up to Johannesburg," Bob told me. "We've had a hell of a battle, but the future's tremendous. Jim's waiting for us in Johannesburg."

I looked through the first four numbers of *Drum* that had already appeared. It was a sixpenny monthly magazine, written in English, printed on cheap yellow newsprint; the bright cover showed two Africans facing each other, symbolically, across the continent: one in a Western hat and suit, the other with African skins and assegai.

The first numbers contained African poems and stories; articles on "Music of the Tribes" and "Know Yourselves", recounting the history of the Bantu tribes; instalments of *Cry, the Beloved Country*; features about religion, farming, sport and famous men; and strip cartoons about Gulliver and St. Paul.

There was a poem by the American negro poet, Countee Cullen:

What is Africa to me?
Copper Sun or Scarlet Sea,
Jungle Star or Jungle Track
Strong bronze men, or regal black
Women from whose loins I sprang
When the birds of Eden sang? . . .

This was *Drum*'s Africa: it was as exotic and exciting as I had hoped Africa to be, unspoilt by the drabness of the West. In one early number there was a Zulu poem called "Mlung ungazikhohlisi"—"White man, do not deceive yourself":

If I pretend to be like you, Prince
Apeing you, I know what I am about
I know what I brought with me
I know what I will take away with me
I know well what is my gourd
How could I forget, this is my birthright
White man, do not deceive yourself . . .

Letters to the editor were enthusiastic about this new African *Drum*:

"Not until I read your magazine," wrote Mr. Zondi from Natal, "and read that beautiful poem by an American negro had I known that the American negroes still long for Africa. I thought that, Americanised and mechanised, they were thankful to be oblivious of the 'Dark, Dark Continent'. But Africa is there deep in their loins never to be forgotten."

Europeans, too, welcomed this new cultural outlet for Africans, which told them of their own traditions and art. The Government sent copies to their information offices abroad, as an example of Bantu achievement.

"Antonio, this *Drum*, it is a wonderful idea!" said Elena,

Bob's intellectual Italian secretary. "It must continue! It is giving the African people what they need . . ."

After a week in Cape Town, Bob and I drove to Johannesburg, nine hundred miles north-east. Johannesburg. Six thousand feet above the sea. Seventy years old, and before that nothing. The second biggest city in Africa, and by far the richest. No river, no lake, no sea within four hundred miles. Only gold, a mile below it, and everything that gold can buy. Fast, tough, rich, vulgar, new, and proud of it. A million people, half white, half black, one half fearing the other.

We moved into two small offices in the middle of Johannesburg. The staff consisted of Bob, his secretary and me, together with an African sports editor who had just been appointed, called Henry Nxumalo; I awaited Henry's arrival anxiously—he would be the first African I had met.

Henry came into the office with a quick jaunty walk. He was a dapper little man, with a fine African head—deep brow, high cheekbones, and a strong mouth. Unlike the lazy story-book negro, he had quick movements and wide intelligent eyes.

We shook hands across the gulf of continents and colour, trying to size each other up. What suspicion and subterfuge was there, I wondered, behind that friendly laugh and those sophisticated manners? Why had this Oxford Englishman come out? no doubt he wondered; what did he want out of Africa, and how long would he continue shaking hands?

"Of course, you come from England?" said Henry. "I loved England when I was there in the war: I made lots of friends."

In the next few days we talked for hours. Henry told me about his life.

"My grandfather was an ordinary tribal Zulu with three wives; he died mysteriously by falling off a cliff. People said he was bewitched, but my father said he was drunk."

Henry's father had died while he was still at school, and he had to support himself by working for the white fathers at the

18

institution. When he left school, he worked as a kitchen boy in Durban. He hated it, ran away, and reached Johannesburg, the goal of all ambitious Africans. He found a job as "boy" in a boilermaker's shop, at fifty shillings a month; in his spare time he wrote poetry for the weekly *Bantu World*.

The *Bantu World* offered him a job as a messenger, and he worked there for three years, rising to be sports writer. He made friends with a young Coloured poet, called Peter Abrahams, and together they discussed how to reform the world.

The war came, and Henry joined the army—not as a soldier, for Africans were forbidden to carry arms, but as a camp-follower. Natives who could read, write and type were rare, and after three days Henry was a sergeant.

He was posted to Cairo, where he made friends with Egyptian students and journalists, and glimpsed a world beyond his dreams. From there he was transferred to England. He forgot about "European Only" and apartheid, and spent his week-ends with English friends. He drank in pubs with the small band of African intellectuals in London, who included his old friend Peter Abrahams, now a struggling author settled in England.

The South African army were alarmed by a native N.C.O. mixing with left-wing intellectuals. First, they restricted Henry's movements in England, then sent him back to South Africa. Soon afterwards, he was demobilised, and found himself a Kaffir again, living in a world of non-Europeans only. He came back to Johannesburg, and married a pretty young African nurse.

He returned to the *Bantu World* as a sports writer, and earned extra money by writing for the American negro *Pittsburg Courier*. But after his glimpse of a wider world, Henry felt frustrated and embittered in his narrow province.

He left to work on a goldmine; then to do welfare work for the British Empire Service League. In his spare time he wrote articles for European papers, such as "How Natives Regard Lightning".

From there, Henry joined the *Drum*; so that I found myself talking to him in the office, where our two very different worlds touched. Henry was the first of many shocks *Drum* gave me: his civilised conversation, laughter, warmth and charm destroyed at one blow many of the misgivings I had entertained about the dark continent. Above all, Henry was enormously human.

Jim Bailey, who was financing the *Drum*, was waiting for us in Johannesburg. He was less sanguine than Bob about the future of the magazine.

"It's all very nice, but the fact is, Africans aren't buying it: the circulation is only twenty thousand. In the meantime, I'm losing two thousand pounds a month."

Our agents were pessimistic: "We've seen so many new magazines come and go."

Why weren't Africans buying it? Henry took Jim, Bob and myself round to African homes and clubs, and we talked unendingly about *Drum*.

"Ag, why do you dish out that stuff, man?" said a man with golliwog hair in a floppy American suit, at the Bantu Men's Social Centre. "Tribal music! Tribal history! Chiefs! We don't care about chiefs! Give us jazz and film stars, man! We want Duke Ellington, Satchmo, and hot dames! Yes, brother, anything American. You can cut out this junk about kraals and folk-tales and Basutos in blankets—forget it! You're just trying to keep us backward, that's what! Tell us what's happening right here, man, on the Reef!"

He summed up the views of most of our non-readers. "Of course, I'm not very interested in tribal music myself," said Henry.

We talked to Job Rathebe, a suave African undertaker and boxing promoter, who had introduced Henry to *Drum*.

"I can tell you what's wrong with *Drum*," he said in an

authoritative drawl, picked up from a visit to the States some years before. "You see, it's got the white hand on it—that's what I call it. *Drum*'s what white men want Africans to be, not what they are. Now, take this tribal history business, which you call 'Know Yourselves': we all know ourselves quite well enough, Mr. Bailey, I assure you. And we're trying to get away from our tribal history just as fast as we can. We don't want *Drum* to remind us. What we want, you see, is a paper which belongs to us—a real *black* paper. We want it to be our *Drum*, not a white man's *Drum*."

Africans hated the "white hand". They suspected every African paper of being a white man's trick to keep them quiet. "A dog with a bone in his mouth can't bark," says a Shangaan proverb. The only paper for Africans which had their confidence was the *Guardian*[1], an outspoken Communist weekly.

Drum was at cross-purposes with its readers. While we were preaching tribal culture and folk-tales, they were clamouring to be let in to the Western world.

Looking back on it now, it seems odd that we could ever have expected Africans to buy the early *Drum*. But the tribal *Drum* was part of a very general attitude of Europeans towards the African in his tribal state. The laughing Zulu or the fierce Masai[2] was the heir of the "noble savage" of Rousseau, Defoe or Lord Monboddo:

BOSWELL: Lord Monboddo still maintains the superiority of
    savage life.
JOHNSON: What strange narrowness of mind now is that, to
    think the things that we have not known, are better than
    the things which we have known.

[1] Later banned, and reappeared successively as the *Clarion*, *People's World*, *Advance* and (at the time of writing) *New Age*.
[2] For the European's admiration of the Masai in Kenya, one of the most backward tribes in Africa, see Elspeth Huxley, *Sorcerer's Apprentice*.

To the white man, the tribal African was a symbol of all that Western man had lost in his long breaking-in down the centuries: he was an image of the lost golden age of childhood.[1] It seemed tragic that he should wish to exchange his carefree tribal life for slums and juke-boxes.

"I like the old native in the reserves; he's a natural gentleman," Europeans would say. "It's these half-educated creatures in the towns that I can't do with."

But to the African, the reserves were impoverished, stagnant and backward; the new Africa lay in the white men's cities, and the white men's ways. *Drum*'s future lay with the "half-educated creatures", in a world less evocative, less mysterious, but far more vital. The jungle track was a dead end.

* * *

Jim was convinced that if *Drum* was to continue, it must be drastically changed; but Bob was loath to abandon the romantic tribal *Drum*. On this and other points there was increasing disagreement between editor and proprietor until, in November, Bob left.

Jim asked me to become editor of the *Drum*, and I accepted.

I could never forget that without Bob's courage and persistence, *Drum* would never have existed. His vision had seen the need and the possibility of a great African paper, to span the continent. However much *Drum* changed its character in the following years, it never lost Bob's original enthusiasm and vision.

[1] For a penetrating study of the psychological significance of the "noble savage," see O. Mannoni, *Psychologie de la Colonisation*. Editions de Seuil, 1950.

CHAPTER TWO

Black Hand

Drum needed the black hand upon it. To compensate for our own whiteness, Jim and I decided to appoint an African editorial board to advise us on policy. They met once a month at lunch-time in my small office, perched on the edge of tables and desks, munching sandwiches and sipping milk between the arguments. I sat back listening to them talking about *their Drum*, too worked up to worry about the susceptibilities of white men.

There was the indefatigable Job Rathebe, bustling in always late, on his way from one important meeting to another. "J. R." was jealous of his African *Drum*, and could detect a white fingerprint anywhere.

"You see, we want it to be our *Drum*. . . . Mr. Sampson, we Africans are very suspicious of the white man: we're used to his promises. . . . Now what about this cover?" standing up and waving our last cover showing a black Santa Claus, which was my special pride: "What's Father Christmas got to do with Africans? There's no snow in December here; Santa Claus doesn't mean anything to us, you know!"

There was Dan "Sport" Twala, "the most popular man on the Reef", bouncing in with his well-pressed suit and neat bow-tie, his large shiny face creased in a huge grin, and his eyes laughing as he spoke. Dan the sportsman, Dan the broadcaster, Dan the socialite, Dan the compere, Dan the film star—everybody's Dan, and now *Drum*'s Dan.

"What's wrong with Father Christmas? I don't see why he should always be white: the whites can't have all the fun, you know!" bursting into a high-pitched guffaw, and pushing over his neighbour in relish of the joke. "But sport's the thing, man!" he said, suddenly grave, as Africans are when they discuss sport. "The boys are screaming for more sport! D'you know, man, I can get a bigger crowd for my Baloyi cup final than any politician, true as God! And if the players don't turn up they lynch me, or stone my house—they do!" And Dan was convulsed with laughter again, remembering his house being stoned.

There was Dr. Alfred Xuma, a diminutive but dignified figure, with distinguished grey hair, and a high forehead above his quick and piercing eyes. He had taken his degree in America, been President of the African National Congress, built up a successful practice, and was now doyen of African politicians. He would walk in solemnly and stiffly, and talk as if to a meeting of presidents, eating his sandwiches between speeches with quiet dignity.

"It is very impor-tant that *Drum* should be completely accurate in everything it publishes," he said with deliberation, with the lilting accent of the Xhosas, pausing in the middle of long words for emphasis. He looked at me accusingly from under his furrowed brows. "There were three inacc-urac-ies in your article on Profess-or Zacharias Matthews which I noticed immediately I read it."

There was Andy Anderson, a Falstaffian Coloured printer, sometimes called "the government printer" because he printed pamphlets for Congress. He would arrive straight from his printing shop in an inky shirt.

"Excuse me, gentlemen, excuse me. We capitalists are busy men, aren't we, Mr. Bailey?" winking at Jim and laughing. He would set in to the sandwiches, nodding, smiling or looking serious according to what was being said. "Hell, that was a terrific girl you had on your last cover!" he would say solemnly. "What we need is more babes like that. I haven't got time to read the stories—I just want to look at the pictures. But, gee, everyone's talking about that babe! How did you find her? And why don't you have some Basuto girls?"

"This picture of a girl dressed up as a cowboy—I don't see the point of it. What does it mean?" asked J.R. "It doesn't mean anything, man!" said Dan. "It's just fun, that's all—she's a cowgirl!" roaring with laughter. "Why is there nothing about Coloureds?" said Andy. "We're sick of Jake Tuli," said J.R.— and so on. "That's too patronising." . . . "Why do you say garden *boy*, when he's a man of fifty?" . . . "We don't like 'Negress'—it sounds like tigress, and you don't talk about 'Europeaness.'" . . . "I can tell a white man wrote *that* bit." . . . "Kindly print Coloured with a capital C." . . . "Why don't you put 'Mr.' in front of my name when you write to me?" . . . "The next magazine you start should be called *Us*." . . . "*Drum* must have *jazz*! You can't have an African paper without jazz!" . . .

The sedate syntax of the European papers was all wrong for our readers, who thought and spoke in jazz and exclamation marks. There was rhythm throbbing in everything they said and did, which no humdrum city life could stamp out. I could see it on posters advertising dances and parties, stuck on lamp-posts and street walls, printed in a glorious mix-up of Victorian types, with exclamation marks worn with use.

BANG! BANG!! BANG!!!
Can you jive? Can you bebop?
Come one, come all to a
GRAND JIVE SESSION!
Ebony Calling!

We wanted *Drum* to have an African style, and to capture some of the vigour of African speech; but it was not easy, for African intellectuals and writers, cut off from their own people, used long words and paraded dry facts, to show off their learning.

Henry brought along a friend called Todd Matshikiza, to

review records. Todd played the piano for the Harlem Swingsters, and composed jazz and choral music. He was a short, neat, little man with a bullet head and a small face which was wrinkled with laughing. He strode into the office on his short legs, his whole frame tense with life; he talked non-stop, with boundless enthusiasm, his big mouth opening and shutting like a ventriloquist's dummy.

"Shucks, I've never written reviews before!" said Todd. "Gee, do you think I could do it? Hell, it's worth having a shot, man! But, gosh, I've never written *anything* before, you know that? I'm a jazz man, not a journalist!"

Todd transformed *Drum*. He wrote as he spoke, in a brisk tempo with rhythm in every sentence. He attacked the type-writer like a piano. Our readers loved "Matshikese", as we called it, which was the way they talked and thought, beating in time with the jazz within them.

Todd wrote about a jazz composer, King Force:

"He stood with his two legs wide apart, his feet firmly on the floor as if holding something down. His head was thrown back and his eyes shut tight as a pot lid. Cheeks blown to bursting to hold that blue note. Wilson Silgee was leading the famous Jazz Maniacs through yet another night of fame.

"In the great days of 'Zulu Boy' Cele, the 1930s, he was a tall, slender, young fellow. A big-eyed floydoy of a jazz maniac. Rushing himself into admiration and fame. Girls. Men. People. Jazz fans. They soon chucked his real name on one side and gave him King Force. A mighty mass of black jazz that was bursting out through every jazz house in Africa. King Force. A power that made you stop plumb dead and beat your chest and cry aloud with the jazz force that his tenor horn was giving.

"On one side of the stage stood another fling-dong, Vy Nkosi, the trombone that rocks tremors into the bowels of the earth.

"Yes, man, those were the power-pillars that held the great Jazz Maniacs together. King Force would say: 'Take it, Vy.' Vy stands up and pulls his trombone to the very last breath. Vy sits down. Wilson (King Force) Silgee ups and takes the solo that makes the dance for the night.

"Twenty years they begged him to put his music on discs. Twenty years he refused. He wanted to carry his message across personally. He's carried that message through more than 50,000 miles of jazz entertainment in South Africa. And now he's put his music, his great sounds, down on Gallotone discs. 'King Force and his Jazz Forces.'

"Funny. It's always these tiny little places that produce these greats. Who would say King Force came from Thaba 'Nchu? I hear you asking: 'Where's Thaba 'Nchu?'

"Jo'burg has claimed him now, as it claims most of the jazz greats. There's a reason too. A quarter of a million blacks spend and end their lives in and around Jo'burg. And where so much life is found, good jazz is found. King Force is found."

*   *   *

"Give us girls, man. . . . Tell us about gangsters. . . . Cut out this tribal stuff. Show us things that *matter*. . . ."

There was no escaping the formula for selling papers: "Cheese cake, crime, animals, babies. . . ." The workers of the world were united, at least, in their addiction to cheese cake and crime. The African's favourite reading was the Overseas *Daily Mirror*. The most popular author in African libraries was Peter Cheyney.

The influence of the city worked fast on tribal Africans, on the surface at least: it soon rubbed out the memories of a slower, gentler life. The Africans born in towns became natural cockneys, revelling in city life, and despising the country.

Drum had, above all, to be human. We had to approach our readers not as a preacher or teacher, but as a colleague. We needed the common touch, which would show readers that *Drum* was one of them.

We took on a young German photographer, Jurgen Schadeberg, who had been brought up in the wild wartime days of bombed Berlin. He combined a strict training in photography with a restless, fearless spirit. He penetrated right inside the African world with his camera, where no photographer had been before, and came back with pictures which summed up the life of Africans in towns: a duel of knives in the middle of a soccer match; liquor-sellers fighting with police; socialites in evening-dress, waltzing in a shack; frenzied spectators at a boxing-match, carrying the champ on their shoulders. The office was invaded by beauty queens and glamour girls, posed in exotic costumes against canvas clouds, while messenger boys wolf-whistled. The dusky beauty of Africa was an almost untouched field of photographs; with her wide brown eyes and flashing white teeth against her smooth bronzed face, she was an exciting subject; and there was opportunity to set a new style of beauty.

For an African paper, we needed African journalists. One day Father Huddleston, the Superintendent of St. Peter's School, asked us if we had a job for a schoolboy, Arthur Maimane, who had a passion for journalism. Arthur was bumptious and outspoken, with a quick wit; he showed me a short story he had written, in slick American dialogue, about American fighter pilots. He was the white man's "cheeky Kaffir"—what happens when you start educating them; but good Kaffirs made bad journalists. We took him on as a cub reporter. He looked the complete Hollywood journalist; he wore a stetson on the back of his head, and a light raincoat slung over his shoulders; he dressed carefully and immaculately, with a bow-tie and dark shirt, a light gaberdine suit, and pointed brown and white shoes. He typed fast, with a cigarette in the corner of his mouth, and barked over the telephone in staccato sentences.

He said what he thought, or more, in his determination not to be servile to white men.

28

"It makes me boil having to say 'Ya, baas' to a white man who's inferior to me," he said. "God, I feel sick when I see an educated African grovelling in front of a white man."

Arthur was completely detribalised. Johannesburg was his universe, and tribal life disgusted him: he hated being mistaken for an "ordinary native" by whites. He was determined to be Western and cosmopolitan, and spent his time with Indian, Coloured and European friends. African nationalism bored him. He wrote slick stories about African detectives, and romances in the locations. His heroes wore big hats, and drove big cars, and talked in racy dialogue.

We began to approach a black *Drum*. Readers proposed to our cover girls, workers talked about our crime exposures in the buses and trains, and illiterate letters to the editor showed that we had attracted people who could barely read. Our readers were human after all.

As we expected, as we gained black admirers, we lost white. "How can you publish such trash?" said Elena, Bob's old secretary, when I saw her again. Subscriptions were cancelled, missionaries complained and schools stopped their orders. But circulation went up.

"*Drum*'s pretty awful," a white liberal said; "but it's important, because it's *human*."

"Come out to my home in Orlando," said Henry one day. We drove out in the evening, through the dingy southern suburbs of Johannesburg, and past the scrap heaps and junk yards at the edge of the town. Henry gave a racy commentary:

"Now we're coming to the Crown Mines, where I used to work as a 'boy'. You see this sign—'Natives Cross Here'? That's where I used to cross. One day someone added the word 'very'—to say 'Natives Very Cross Here!' . . . And here are the mine dumps! You know, when the Zulus and Basutos come to Johannesburg for the first time, they think those are real

29

gold! They say, 'Eeeeee! Look at the gold mountains!' . . . And here's Baragwanath hospital—it's one of the biggest hospitals in Africa: all for natives! That's where Florence, my wife, works. . . . Over there, there's a cemetery for non-Europeans. Of course, it's very apartheid, even when you're dead! The natives are kept away from the Coloureds. . . . Look! You can see Orlando now, on the hill there!"

Over the dark-brown hillside was a pattern of little red blobs in rows; above the township lay a pall of smoke, and in the twilight the houses were dark and dead.

"No electricity?" I asked.

"Of course, natives don't need light! We call this the 'Dark City'. Or sometimes we call it London. Or New York! We call it anything."

We stopped at the Orlando filling station for petrol. We beckoned the African attendant, who came up and made a comic salute.

"Yes, my lord?" And he gave Henry a queer look, seeing him in the front of the car.

"Tell me, do you read a magazine called the *Drum*?"

"Drummer? Yes, baasie, always drummer. Good magazine. Good drummer."

"Do you like the pictures? Or the stories?"

"Good pictures, good stories. Very good, baasie."

Henry spoke to him in Zulu, and he nodded his head knowingly and said, "Aaaaah." Henry said:

"He hasn't the slightest idea what we're talking about. He's just a clot! . . ."

We drove on. ". . . Now we're in Orlando, the African city. They call it a model location, but I don't know what they mean. You see that long, low building there, with all the smoke coming out? That's called the Shelters. It's a row of little rooms, with one tap at the end of each row. . . . And you see that two-storey house just next to them? It's the only two-storey house in

30

Orlando. It belongs to a—*witch doctor*." Henry whispered the word mysteriously, and laughed.

I looked round at the rows of small box houses, like a giant chicken farm. Henry guided me through the dark labyrinthine roads, which degenerated into dirt-track. "This is Orlando West, where the—mind that ditch—big noises live, like me. That's right, across the railway line—there's no train coming. . . . There are some gangsters, looking for someone to rob. . . . There's the six-fifty, just left." And I saw a swarm of Africans running down the bank from the station, with their hats, umbrellas and brief-cases, like any other suburban traveller, but with more gaiety and less dignity.

"Look out for that rock. . . . That funny-looking building there is a church. Oh, Bantu Christian Zionist Baptist Episcopal, or something. There's one church where every member is a bishop, you know. Now we're coming to my house, across this bit of veld here, but be careful of the pit. Here we are."

It was like travelling back a century, across treacherous roads, to this desolate city. Only ten miles out of Johannesburg, this was a new kind of darkest Africa.

Henry led me into a small room, lit by a paraffin lamp. I looked round at the polished furniture, the carpets, piano and armchairs, in unconcealed surprise. We were back in Europe.

Some friends of Henry's arrived, and talked. They were all detribalised African cockneys, born and bred on the Reef. They had a gift for talk, which came more naturally than silence—a relaxed and casual talk, flickering with mimicry and humour and gentle irony, dancing on the edge of bitterness. They talked dramatically and expressively, with a Latin use of gestures, and if they were not talking they listened with devouring eyes, murmuring the long African aaaaah! or eeeeee! in sympathy with the story-teller. They talked about people, with a minute perception of idiosyncrasy or pretence, yet with the broad humanity and tolerance of a race which cannot afford to be

31

intolerant. They noticed how people walked, or coughed, or repeated expressions, or twiddled their fingers or puffed at cigarettes; and their own conversation seemed to take fire in a blaze of extravagance and comedy.

Todd came in, and thumped jazz from the piano, as he said, "drowning the sorrows of nine million black voices". Everyone sang, or wailed, or beat time; the thin walls seemed to melt with the music. Music and people were the only things that mattered. People were the furniture, the wireless, the books, the gramophone.

As I saw more of the world of townee Africans, I lost my disappointment over the failure of the tribal *Drum*, and the black man's aping of white ways. For they were still African, in a deeper sense than blankets and skins: their vigour, jazz and warm laughter belonged to the youth of the world.

I met Africans from every walk of life, whose European equivalents I would never have occasion to meet. The barrier of colour was so great that, once crossed, all other frontiers seemed unimportant. I found freedom of movement among Africans which I could never have among my own race. Across the barrier, I could mix with gangsters, musicians, bus drivers, delivery boys, film stars, boxers. . . .

I realised that, as editor of an African magazine, I had an opportunity, nearly unique, to penetrate the African world. I had an excuse and a passport to know Africans, not as a teacher, but as a pupil.

CHAPTER THREE

House of God

Picture features, bright covers, jazz, girls, and crime stories pushed *Drum*'s circulation up to thirty-five thousand. But Jim and I were disappointed. *Drum* was still below its rival, *Zonk*, a picture magazine for Africans. There was still a fog of suspicion between *Drum* and its readers, and we were far from being accepted as a black paper. "It's just a white's propaganda sheet. Why else would any white man run a paper for Africans?" We heard many stories from Africans about the ownership.

"Of course it belongs to the Chamber of Mines, man."

"Don't you know? It's run by the Colonial Office."

"You can't fool us—everyone knows you're a British spy."

We had to show, powerfully, that *Drum* was for, and not against, its readers.

One day in the office Henry said:

"By the way, have you heard of a place called Bethal?" casually, in the way that he introduced his most startling disclosures. "It's a farming district in the Eastern Transvaal, where they grow potatoes. Of course, there's a good deal of flogging goes on there. . . ."

"Flogging?"

"Yes, it's rather very famous for the way the white farmers beat up the African workers."

"How do you know about Bethal?"

"I went there with the Reverend Scott, three years ago. We looked round some of the farms, and afterwards the Reverend

33

Scott published a report. I suppose it's still the same. Bethal means 'the House of God'." He laughed.

I asked Henry to find out more about Bethal. He came back with a file of press cuttings. We looked through them.

1929: a farmer of Bethal (Rex v. Nafte) was found guilty of tying a labourer by his feet from a tree, and flogging him to death, pouring scalding water into his mouth when he cried for water.

1944: a labourer at Bethal was beaten to death for attempting to escape (Rex v. Johannes Mahlangu).

1944: a labourer was beaten to death (Rex v. Isaac Sotetshi).

1947: a farmer assaulted two labourers, set his dog on them, flogged them and chained them together for the night.

1947: a farm foreman was found guilty of striking a labourer with a whip and setting his dog on him.

1947: a foreman was found guilty of ill-treating African labourers. . . .

And so the list continued. It was a glimpse of another Africa.

We had a conference. Everyone had heard stories about Bethal.

"I've got a cousin in Pretoria who went there," said Arthur. Next day he went to Pretoria, and came back with his cousin's story. I read through it.

"Three years ago, I had been looking for work in Pretoria for two months, when one day I met a white baas in the street. He said that he knew a baas who wanted boys to work on his lorry, going to Johannesburg. This, I thought, would be wonderful work, and I would see the City of Gold. He told me to go to an office in Church Street.

"There I found this baas. He told me that he did not have any more work for lorry boys, but he had work on his farm. . . . After you walk the streets for nine weeks, you are glad for any work, I told him I would work for him.

"I was taken to the yard behind, where I found six other men.

34

We spent three days there, and were not allowed to go out. On the fourth day, we were marched into an office, and after some writing by the white men we were told to hold a pen in the hand. After we had all done this we were told that we had signed a contract for six months' work on this white man's farm. This alarmed us, and we asked to be cancelled. The baas said we could rub our signatures off with money only. We had no money, so we climbed into the canvas-covered light lorry with the others. We climbed out of it with cramped legs that night in Leslie (near Bethal). We were led into a compound surrounded by a high stone wall, given a blanket each, and told to sleep in one of the low, dirty, mud-walled rooms by a black foreman.

"At dawn on the Monday we were herded into the fields by black and white men, riding horses and carrying sjambohks. The black guards were telling us, 'Le jele nama ea Kalajane, kajeno le tla e patela.' 'You have eaten the meat of a cheat and today you will pay for it.' We did not understand that we were to pay for the meat of Kalajane with burning stripes on our backs.

"We strung out in a straight line from one end of the potato field to the other, holding bags and big baskets between us. We were not to break the line or we would be whipped by the guards. We were not to leave any potatoes behind or we would be whipped. It was difficult for us to keep in line without leaving some potatoes behind, and our backs were not used to this prolonged bending, so we were constantly whipped and cursed.

"At midday we had a meal of dry, stiff porridge that looked like white clods of earth as it lay on the bags. In the evening we were herded back to the compound, walking on tired feet, with bent backs. After the porridge we lay down on the blocks of cement and slept like the dead must sleep . . .

"One day the police came to the farm. We were called before them, and they asked us if we were satisfied with the conditions. For a moment nobody answered. Then some said, 'Yebo Nkosi' ('Yes, my lord'). My heart was filled with anger at this untruth, but I knew why they had said it. They hoped to curry favour with the white men. Nobody could dare to contradict what they had said, for they would have paid most sorely for that moment of boldness . . ."

So the story went on. He had his arm broken when a lump of earth was thrown at him by a guard; soon after that he broke a plough. To pay for the plough, he had to stay on three months after his contract. At last, nine months after he had left Pretoria, he was free again. "It seemed a dream of joy from which I would wake any moment," he said, "when I climbed down from the train in Pretoria station."

Most Bethal labourers were working under a contract, like Arthur's cousin; they had been recruited in all sorts of odd ways, by special agencies with names like "African's Guardian". Some were tricked into signing a contract which they did not understand. Some were offered a contract at Bethal as an alternative to being jailed for being without a pass in Johannesburg. Some were picked up near the Rhodesian border, on their way to the Golden City, and threatened with arrest for illegal entry unless they signed a contract. Other labourers were convicts, transferred from the overcrowded Reef jails to one of the seven "farm jails" built by farmers in the Bethal area, and sent to work on the farms, where they were locked and guarded in compounds, and watched and flogged to make them work. Every week, several labourers tried to escape from Bethal.

The contract system, under which labourers were bound to their employers for six months or more, was the root of the trouble. Under law, Africans who broke their contract could be severely punished; but the government could not properly supervise the conditions of contract labourers. The very fact that farmers had to rely on contract labour showed that conditions could not attract the normal casual worker.

The Diocesan Synod of the Anglican Church had issued a memorandum as early as October, 1944:

It must be clear that the extension of the mine compound system to farms without any of the safeguards against the exploitation of the labourer is leading to the kind of exploitation characteristic of the Industrial Revolution in Europe.

Bethal had become a name of terror to Africans. Bethal lorries had to change the notorious "TAB" number-plates when they picked up recruits. Recruits for Bethal were told they were going to Springs or Nigel, and then redrafted to Bethal. A labourer, Frank Phivi, jumped out of a train when he heard it was going to Bethal, and killed himself.

I showed the facts about Bethal to Jim. Himself a farmer with fifty African labourers, he felt strongly about farm conditions.

"Don't you think *Drum* should visit Bethal?" I asked. Jim agreed.

"I'd better go there and have a look," said Henry, grinning. "When shall I go?"

Henry went off to Bethal, raggedly dressed like a farm labourer. After his previous visit with Michael Scott, he already knew his way around. After two days, I had a call from him.

"I've seen quite a lot. Can you send Mr. Schadeberg to meet me here at Bethal? I've got some things to show him." Jurgen went off to join Henry.

I waited anxiously in the office. After four days, Henry came back, tired and unkempt, and typed out his story.

He had travelled all over the Bethal area; he had visited eight different farms and talked to fifty labourers. He and Jurgen had used various ruses: sometimes they were a visiting journalist and his "boy", interested in agricultural problems; sometimes they had simply lost their way. While a farmer was proudly showing off a model building, Jurgen quickly turned round and took a picture of a barbed-wire compound; while Jurgen heard a lecture about the excellent farm conditions, Henry chatted quietly to the African labourers. Often the farmers were quite friendly. One genial farmer, notorious as a slave driver, presented Henry, the "well-mannered native", with a sack of potatoes to take home. Once, they were caught red-handed snooping round a compound by an angry farmer, and had to race for the car.

Of the fifty labourers Henry talked to, not one was satisfied with his conditions. Thirty-two said they had been tricked into coming to Bethal.

Joseph, who said he was fourteen years old, told me he was recruited in the Northern Transvaal, to work in a clothing factory at Springs. He was given an advance of 10s. for food and a train ticket, only to discover at Springs that he was going to work at a farm in Bethal for £2 a month. . . . Mzuzumi said he was recruited in Natal and told he would work in Johannesburg. His party was made to alight at Bethal Station in the dead of night. . . .

The workers told Henry stories about the cruelty of farmers like "Mabulala" (The killer), and "Fakefutheni" (Hit him in the marrow). One told him how he had been made to bury secretly a fellow worker who had been flogged to death. Henry talked to an African in Bethal Hospital, Casbert Tutje, who had been admitted after he was thrashed by his boss for attending a beer-drinking party on Christmas day.

Jurgen took a picture of one of the high-walled compounds with barbed wire round the top, and the bare rooms inside with concrete ledges for beds. "Most of the compounds I saw," said Henry, "looked much like jails: they have high walls, they are dirty, and are often so close to a cattle kraal that the labourers breathe nearly the same air as the cattle."

Jurgen's pictures confirmed everything we had heard: there were the bruised hands of Joseph, the fourteen-year-old boy; labourers eating dry porridge off filthy sacks; a boss boy on horseback, carrying a long whip, with the labourers walking in front of him; the long line of potato pickers, carrying sacks between them, as Arthur's cousin had described them.

Our story was nearly complete; but we still had to check the method of recruiting labourers for Bethal.

"How do you think we can see people being recruited?" I said to Henry.

"By the way, I suppose I could get recruited myself," said Henry. "It's easy enough to get signed on, and I'm sure I can get out of it at the last minute...."

Next morning Henry, shabbily dressed, walked off to the Johannesburg Pass Office. Hundreds of Africans were queuing as usual round the building, trying to obtain passes which would allow them to stay in Johannesburg. Others lingered about looking for work, or hoping to pick up forged passes. Henry waited until he saw a smart African tout trying to conscript Africans to work on the farms, and followed him.

"Say, what's the matter, brother?" said the tout, noticing him.

"I've got no pass, man!"

"Say, you've hit the right guy!" said the tout, sniffing a five-bob commission. "I'll take you to a baas who'll get you a pass if you work for him...."

Henry went happily off with the tout to an employment agency round the corner, where a white man told him he would have to work outside Johannesburg. Henry gave him his name as George Magwaza, and was taken to a filthy compound nearby, where he spent the night with scores of Africans without passes.

Next morning, Henry was paraded with fifty other recruits in front of the government-appointed "attesting officer". In front of the officer was a large contract sheet; an African clerk called the names of all the recruits on the sheet, and then gabbled:

"You're going to work on a farm in the Middelburg district;

you're on a six-months' contract. You will be paid three pounds
a month, plus food and quarters. When you leave here you will
be given an advance of 5s. for pocket money, 10s. 5d. for food,
and 14s. 5d. for train fare. The total amount is £1. 9s. 10d., and
this amount will be deducted from your first month's wages.
Have you got that?"

"Yes," they said.

"You will now proceed to touch the pencil," said the clerk.

"But I was told before that I was going to be sent to a farm
in Springs," Henry piped up. "Why am I now going to
Middelburg?"

"I'm telling you where you're going, according to your
contract sheet, and nothing else," said the clerk brusquely.

The attesting officer then held a pencil above the contract
sheet, and the fifty recruits ran past him, touching the pencil as
they passed. But when Henry reached the attesting officer, he
refused to touch the pencil. He was told to wait outside for his
pass, and went away. On his way out he managed to pick up a
copy of a contract sheet, and brought it back to the office.

The above Contract of Service [it said at the bottom] was
read aloud, interpreted and fully explained to the above-
mentioned natives, who acknowledged that they understood
the same and voluntarily affixed their signatures (or marks)
thereto in my presence. . . .

The number of natives attested on this Contract sheet
is. . . . .

. . . .
ATTESTING OFFICER

The next day, Henry went back to the recruiting office with
Jurgen. They found a window which looked into the room
where the pencil-touching was taking place. Jurgen flashed his
camera as a man touched the pencil, and ran.

Our story was complete.

For *Drum*'s first birthday, in March, 1952, we published an eight-page article called "Bethal Today". We carefully limited our attack to Bethal farms and the contract system. We outlined Bethal's record of flogging and torture, quoted the story of Arthur's cousin, and gave Henry's account, written under the name of "Mr. Drum", of his visit to Bethal and to the recruiting agency. Opposite the story were Jurgen's photographs of compounds and farm labourers, and the recruit touching the pencil.

Die Transvaler, the Nationalist daily paper controlled by Hans Strijdom, now Prime Minister, noticed the article immediately. "The article is written to stir up trouble and cause ill-feeling." The *Rand Daily Mail* followed next day with a long extract from the article. "We are satisfied," they said in an editorial, "that what the magazine *Drum* has said about labour conditions in the Bethal area is substantially correct."

Senator Ballinger, one of the three "Natives' Representatives", raised the question in Parliament the following day.

"Do you not consider it necessary to appoint a Royal Commission?" he asked Dr. Verwoerd, the Minister of Native Affairs.

"I regard the article in *Drum* as being a most unjust attack," replied the minister, "by unwarranted generalisations and by causing unproved deductions to be made. . . ."

He went on to say that a special investigator had been appointed a year before to inspect farms in the Eastern Transvaal; his reports showed that the rules laid down by the government had not been broken.

"My reply clearly shows," he concluded, "that there is no need for an enquiry."

The Bethal number sold out. The first urgent request for more supplies came from our agents at Bethal: we discovered that the Bethal farmers had bought up bulk supplies from the agents, and burnt them, to stop Africans reading them. But they did not succeed. "Bethalians are calling *Drum* 'the emancipating magazine'," wrote an African court interpreter from Bethal, "and every literate of Bethal is buying it."

Letters came from all parts of South Africa with more stories about Bethal.

"My uncle went to Johannesburg to search for work," said a reader from Swaziland. "After three months he sent us a letter without an address saying that he was working for a certain farmer in the Bethal district. Nine months later my uncle returned home penniless. . . . Mr. Editor, he was so emaciated that at first I doubted whether he was the same uncle who had left home young, energetic, stout and handsome. He had a terrible cough and no medicine seemed to do him any good. Two months later he passed away. . . ."

In the meantime Dr. Verwoerd, in spite of the denials, appointed a small committee to visit Bethal and report to him. It included the Director of Native Labour, the farms inspector, a representative from the State Information Office, and a journalist. They asked Henry to accompany them.

The little party set out on their tour of Bethal. Henry pointed out the barbed-wire compounds, the dirty hovels, the rooms next to the cattle kraal. Some of the conditions were worse than we had painted them, some better. Henry nervously re-met the farmers he had seen before in a different role: the farmer who had given him potatoes glowered at him, and presented a sack to the white journalist.

The report was submitted to the minister, but never published. We learnt afterwards that it was more critical than our original article.

The Institute of Race Relations, an impartial academic body, conducted a special investigation. In their report, they stated that in twenty per cent of the cases they examined labourers suffered ill-treatment, sometimes serious. Enough evidence, they considered, had been found to justify an official enquiry.

INSTITUTE CONFIRMS "DRUM'S" STORY, *Die Transvaler* generously reported.

As a result of Mr. Drum's visit, some changes were made at Bethal. Barbed wire was taken down from compounds, and crumbling buildings were ordered to be rebuilt. For a time, at least, recruits were made to sign the contracts instead of touching the pencil, and the contracts were read out fully, in several languages. More important, perhaps, the publicity from the article warned Africans against the dangers of unknown contracts.

But the root of the trouble, the contract system, remained; and with it, remained the abuses. In the next year, the usual court cases came up in Bethal. Two labourers were hung hand-cuffed from the ceiling as punishment; kicking, flogging and chaining continued without much change.

"There'll always be a Bethal," a veteran South African journalist said. "It's a hardy annual—good for a story once a year. . . ."

*   *   *

Though *Drum* did not much change Bethal, Bethal changed *Drum*. "Mr. Drum" caught the imagination of our readers. He was a person, not a magazine; he was one of them. He did things that they did; he was a friend that shared their troubles. In letters and conversation, we could see the beginning of a valuable bond between Mr. Drum and his readers.

"Who is this wonderful Mr. Drum?" "Because of your bravery I suggest calling you Dr. Drum instead of Mr. Drum. In fact, Dr. Bravery would be the most appropriate name for you."

"What adds dignity to *Drum*'s courageous attempt," wrote Thebe Mpulwana, "is the fact that it is not under any political influence whatsoever. The *Drum* has indeed proved itself not only to be a friend and guide of the African, but also a faithful watchdog which guards our heritage with unprecedented alertness. We are all proud of it; we wish it a long and prosperous life in its endeavour to uphold the honour of the African people."

Letters to Mr. Drum asked him to expose conditions in other parts of South Africa, and expected him to continue his crusade.

Jim and I discussed the future of Mr. Drum. Jim was a "liberal" to Africans much as his father had been liberal towards Afrikaners, at a time when most English were as hostile to Boers as Boers were to natives. Jim inherited the goodwill his father had gained among Afrikaner politicians, and had the rare combination of friendships with both Afrikaners and Africans.

We did not want *Drum* to become involved in political agitation, or to develop into a narrow paper of protest. But without exposing scandals of such importance to our readers' lives, the paper would be incomplete and meaningless. Mr. Drum was inevitably launched on a perilous and lonely crusade.

There was no lack of scandals to attack. South Africa was good crusading country. Labour conditions in many places resembled, often closely, the conditions in England a hundred years ago, and the horrors of the Industrial Revolution repeated themselves.

It was possible, too, that our crusades might have some success; for South Africa, unlike some other parts of Africa, was still sensitive to moderate criticism from within.

In the following months, we published a series of articles by Mr. Drum on labour conditions in South Africa. One was about the "tot system" in the vineyards of the Cape, where Coloured workers are paid partly in tots of wine, and live in a haze of semi-drunkenness. Another article dealt with the sugar farms of Natal, where Indian children sometimes earned sixpence for an eight-hour day, and some workers are enslaved by debt to their employers.

The visits to Bethal, the sugar farms, and the tot vineyards, established Mr. Drum as a friend of Africans. *Drum* showed the black hand.

Our circulation responded quickly. A year after Bethal, *Drum*'s sales in South Africa had risen to sixty thousand. Copies were distributed all over English-speaking Africa, and we were established as the leading African paper in the continent.

In gaining support from Africans, we lost it from many Europeans. With Bethal and the exposures that followed, we parted ways with many white allies, and began to find ourselves with embarrassing new supporters, including Communists, African Nationalists and revolutionaries. Between conservatives who considered us seditious, and radicals who considered us frivolous and non-committal, we were in a lonely predicament.

Mr. Drum remained an object of suspicion among Europeans. We pointed out in vain that *Drum* was a bridge—one of the few—between black and white; and that articles like Bethal gave Africans new hope for white justice.

As we lost some supporters in South Africa, so we gained allies in the world outside. The *News Chronicle* and the *Observer* published articles describing *Drum*'s progress.

"Is Sampson black?" cabled *Time* magazine. The following week they wrote:

"*Drum* has . . . become the leading spokesman for South Africa's 9,000,000 negro and Coloured population. In South Africa, torn by racial strife, *Drum*'s popularity is easily explained. 'We air the views and grievances of the blacks,' says the publisher, 'and make them feel that Communism isn't the solution to their problems.' Summed up one white: '*Drum* makes South Africa's segregated, despised non-whites feel like people.'"

"Sixty thousand, and all done by darkies!" shouted Todd, dancing round the office, waving the audited certificate of our circulation. "Shucks, that'll show 'em—a real darkies' paper! But, gee," he said to me, looking serious, "I wish I could find a darky rich enough to buy *Drum*. Then I could sack you and Mr. Bailey."

CHAPTER FOUR

Cheeky Kaffirs

Henry was the presiding spirit in the *Drum* office. With his gay charm, his massive courage, his fits of wild excess and remorse, he was all African. He joked about natives and Kaffirs with bursting laughter, and only occasionally showed a glimpse of the well of bitterness beneath the laugh.

Todd became a full-time member of the staff. I listened to him and Henry talking, exasperated by deadlines overdue, but too absorbed to interrupt.

TODD: Good morning, Captain!

HENRY: 'Morning, Toddy-boy!

TODD: Shucks, Hen, but that was an evening! No! It was! Those Queenstown boys, they're crazy, man! I thought they would die—honestly!

HENRY: By the way, you got home safely? (Chuckle.)

TODD: *I* got home safely? Who are you fooling? And you were jiving round the floor kissing a chair! Remember?

HENRY: Of *course* I don't remember. But you're feeling all right?

TODD: Me? Me? I went on to the Cabin in the Sky. I went on to the Barn. I went on to the Thirty-Nine Steps, with Zig Zag Zakes and the boys screaming "Stop!"

HENRY: Of course, Sis Dhlamini wasn't there?

TODD: She wasn't? Then I wasn't! Shucks, what a sheila! She wore a dress that sent the boys gasping! Wide white stripes round the flare! Running round her body, round her curves,

46

right into my eyes! Gee! Wasn't she there? But how did *you* get here this morning?

HENRY: I'm fine! I'm fine! I was worried about you, that's all. . . . I was afraid you might get into trouble. . . .

TODD: And you! Asleep in the bass drum. Stopping the band. Shouting at the cop. Stopping the car. You!

HENRY: Me? Did I? Funny, I don't remember . . .

*　　　*　　　*

Our staff increased rapidly. *Drum* was to be written entirely by Africans, but it was not easy to build up an African staff: there were few precedents, and no one was qualified. The subservience that other white employers required from their native boys was precisely what we did not want. Judging character across the colour line was doubly difficult. There were no recognisable labels and the tricks and pretences I noticed in my own race fooled me easily among Africans. I knew nothing of the classes of African society, and I caught myself generalising about "the African" as if he were not altogether an individual.

Nonetheless, collecting an African staff was an absorbing problem. We could offer almost unlimited opportunity to anyone who could grasp it; and we had nearly the whole population of four and a half million African men to choose from. Most of the few Africans educated at secondary schools and universities ended up either as teachers or with unimportant jobs in white offices.

Jim and I were determined to employ Europeans only where no African could do their job. Otherwise, *Drum* should be a black firm.

We needed a messenger boy, and Henry brought along a nephew, Bob Gosani, a lanky schoolboy of sixteen. Bob lived in Ferreirastown, a rough slum corner of Johannesburg frequented by thugs, and his father wanted to find him a job to prevent him becoming a gangster.

As a messenger boy, Bob was slow and lazy, and seemed to

embody most of the faults one expected from an African. He would wander disconsolately into my office.

"Mr. Sampson—the thing is—that man—the white man— he wants a copy of *Drum*—he says can I give him one—the thing is—we've not got none left. . . ."

We were debating whether to fire Bob, when Jurgen asked for a dark-room assistant. Bob said he'd like that job, so we tried him out. He took to photography immediately. A year later he was taking half the pictures in *Drum* and later, when Jurgen was away, he took them all. We syndicated his pictures to English and American magazines. He was the only important African photographer in the country. Europeans could not believe that this black boy fiddling with a Rolleiflex was taking real photographs.

As our African staff expanded, *Drum* became a little world of its own. One visitor called it "a little bit of the Gold Coast in South Africa." People referred to "*Drum* Africans" as if they were a separate race.

A man called at the European newspaper office adjoining *Drum*, and asked an African messenger:

"Where's the dark-room?"

"This way, baas!" said the messenger, and trotted round the corner to the *Drum* office; he pointed proudly to the room full of Africans.

"This is the dark room, baas!"

The *Drum* office had a succession of surprised and surprising visitors. One day Dan Choco, then the office boy, came into my office.

"Seven witch doctors to see you, sir."

There they were, lined up against the layout desk, dressed in full regalia—bright headdresses with beads festooned all round, skins over their bodies, elaborate studded belts, gay-decorated skirts, and bangles clanking on their bare arms and legs. Their chief introduced himself in cultured English.

"I am Doctor Khontsiwe, President of the African National Herbalist Association of Newclare. These are members of my board. We wish to complain about the allegations in your last *Drum* that witch doctors are responsible for ritual murders. . . ."

White visitors were usually startled by the *Drum* office, with Africans typing, proof-reading, taking photographs or working the telephone. Once a young reporter from an Afrikaans newspaper arrived to ask for a photograph. He looked round at natives typing.

"Do the—er—natives do the writing for this paper?" he asked an African sub-editor, hesitating to use the word native.[1] He forgot about the photograph, and instead wrote an article about the native magazine, describing how a native editor talked to him in a thickly padded conference room about the policy of the paper, while minions padded in and out with galley proofs and blocks. He ended: "But why isn't there a paper for natives in Afrikaans?"

The relations between our "little bit of the Gold Coast" and the rest of South Africa were often strained. When European painters or carpenters worked in the office, they resented the "cheeky Kaffirs" doing more skilled work than they. One day a white painter was working outside our windows, with a "native boy" to help him according to South African custom—not to paint, but to pass the brush when required, or to haul the platform up and down, or simply to be sworn at. The white man was irritated by watching African journalists through the window, and took it out of his "boy" by shouting at him. The "boy" replied in Zulu, which the white man couldn't understand; but Arthur overheard it. "You white man, you wish you could be in there doing that work, don't you?"

White men knew little about the Africans they worked next

[1] *Naturelle* in Afrikaans: there is no Afrikaans equivalent to *African*, since *Afrikaner* means one of their own white people.

to. I used to hear from my window Africans lifting heavy machinery in the street to the rhythm of traditional chants. One day the Johannesburg municipality announced that they were installing loudspeakers to relay the songs to the workers.

"What they don't realise," one of our staff explained, "is that they're mostly songs of hate against the white man. The most popular one begins 'abelungu goddamn,' which means 'god-damn the white man.'"

In the office, there was always difficulty with the South Africa around us: there was constant pressure from outside to regard all Africans as "boys", and only white men as responsible. "I can't get past this barrage of natives," complained an advertiser. "Mr. van Schalkwyk prefers not to talk to natives on the phone, if you please."

It was amusing watching the reactions of European visitors to the office. At one time we had two postmen, both Afrikaners. One of them always refused to accept African signatures for registered letters, and insisted each time on seeing "the baas". The other, after some reticence at first, would sit down to tea with the African staff and exchange stories.

White visitors would often order editors around as if they were "boys" to run errands. Sometimes advertisers came to the office for information about African buying habits. Having met no Africans except servants, they questioned our editors in baby language.

"You use toothbrush? Eh? Clean teeth? Eh? Like this? . . ." A manufacturer demonstrated to Arthur, waggling his fingers in front of his clenched teeth, and talking loudly, like an Englishman abroad.

"Yes, I use your make of toothbrush," said Arthur; "they're cheaper and better than the others, but I find the bristles too long. . . ."

Some of the jobs on *Drum* had to be done by Europeans; but it was hard to find people in South Africa who would regard working with Africans not as a mission, nor as a Communist plot, but simply as part of a job.

Our greatest trouble was what we called the "battle of the tea-cups". There is an old South African theory that, although you have a native cook in your kitchen, and a native nurse-girl who baths your child, there is something particularly terrible about drinking out of a cup that a native has used. One temporary typist took fright immediately.

"Do you drink out of the same cups as the native boys?" came the old question.

"Oh, no!" said our advertising manager, who had a pile of letters he wanted typed, "we keep them *quite* separate."

"But how do you tell the difference?" she persisted, looking at the cups.

He thought wildly.

"Oh, we wash them up in separate places."

In dealing with our African staff, I felt constantly the pressure from outside, of the strong mythology of race. Voices saying "because he is black", "because he is white". If someone was fired, it was because he was black. If someone promoted, because he was white. In times of crisis, if there was a theft or a row, black and white would retreat to their own camps and glower at each other.

Our world was isolated, and sometimes lonely. Marching perpetually out of step was exhausting. It was a relief when we occasionally had visitors from the world outside South Africa who shared our views. Foreign correspondents and travelling journalists called on *Drum* on their way through Africa, and brought a gust of fresh air into the overcharged atmosphere.

One frequent visitor was Alex Campbell, *Time-Life* correspondent for Africa.

"What's the best place in Africa for a black man to live?" Henry asked Alex.

"Right here in South Africa."

"What? Here?" came a chorus of disbelief.

"What about Rhodesia? There's no colour bar there," said Henry.

"No colour bar? It's all that Malan ever hoped for," said Alex.

"And the Gold Coast! That's a real darkies' country! Shucks, what about Accra?" asked Todd.

"Accra's rather like Sophiatown, without Johannesburg."

"But there's no colour bar."

"Not much money either. . . . It depends which you want, freedom or money."

"Freedom," said Todd.

"Money," said Arthur.

Our most spectacular visitor was Peter Abrahams. He flew in one morning by Comet from London, and cabled for Henry to meet him at the airport.

Peter, now an established writer in London, was on a month's visit to South Africa, after fourteen years away, to write articles for the *Observer*, and broadcasts for the B.B.C.

Henry brought Peter back to the office, where everyone was waiting. Peter was neat and debonair, with a trim moustache and large expressive eyes. He was confident and unhesitating, unlike his African friends, and with no trace of apology. He spoke with a lazy English drawl.

Peter knew Johannesburg well. He was born and brought up in Vrededorp, one of the worst slums in Johannesburg; he earned pennies by carrying bags in the market, dodging the police, and later by working for a smithy for 2s. 6d. a day. He used to gaze through the windows of white houses, at the forbidden world of "Europeans only". When he was eleven, he sent himself to school, discovered poetry and books, and resolved to be a writer. He met white people and wrote poetry and stories. After frustration and disappointment in South Africa, he was taken on as a ship's stoker, and reached England. He made England his home, was accepted and encouraged, and wrote himself out of bitterness into a mature and powerful style. He married an English wife, and most of his friends were Europeans.

But in Johannesburg Peter was a Kaffir again. He could not stay in a hotel, or eat at a restaurant. He lived at home with his mother, a simple Coloured woman.

Peter's impact on his own people after fourteen years was summed up in his relations with Henry, who had once shared so much of his life. The gulf that was now between them saddened them both. Peter had become a successful author, free, confident, his own master expressing himself to the full. Henry had been frustrated, humiliated, hitting himself against a wall. Peter was the image of what might have been.

When later Peter wrote a book about his visit, *Return to Goli*,[1] I asked Henry to review it in *Drum*. "Some of his chapters sound like a Return to Me," wrote Henry. "When I met Peter and piloted him round these troubled parts, he was indeed a new man. He couldn't understand the reasons for all the bitterness between white and black; he was more understanding of the reasons of the attitudes of the whites towards the blacks, and more English than the English themselves. . . ."

Peter was impatient of the bitterness and complexes of his old friends; and he told them so frankly. The Coloured Garment Workers' Union gave a banquet for two hundred people in his honour, and Peter invited me. After the sumptuous meal, well-known Coloured leaders made speeches in his praise. He replied to the toast:

"Why do you waste money on a banquet for me, when you could give a scholarship to make another writer? And why haven't you brought your wives? What's the good of talking about liberation, if you haven't even liberated your own women?"

"He isn't one of us," muttered someone next to me.

To *Drum*, Peter's frankness was invaluable. He was a unique

[1] Faber & Faber, 1953.

bridge. As a black man, he could criticise Africans freely, and see their faults; as a European, he was aloof from bitterness and duplicity. He took a strong interest in *Drum* and its ideals. He attacked Jim, me and Henry alike. He swept away suspicion and misunderstanding, and cleared the air.

"These 'Masterpieces in Bronze' you write, Henry," said Peter in his lofty voice. "Why do you make all Africans out to be angels? Take this man you've just written about: we all know he's an old drunkard—he was before I went to England. It's time Africans started criticising each other.

"As for all this American slang of yours, Arthur, it's just wasting your talents. You should be writing literature, not rubbish. . . .

"And you, Tony," he went on, "you're too sensitive about the susceptibilities of your readers. You should treat 'em rough. Tell them their leaders are lousy and their politicians stink. They need to be criticised. They've got to stop being so touchy. I know. I'm one of them."

The night before he left South Africa, Peter gave a party at his mother's house in Coronationville. All his family were there—his mother, happily pottering in the kitchen, shy in front of Peter's sophisticated friends; his brother, a jovial, toothless labourer, muttering incomprehensible jokes half in Afrikaans; his sister Maggie, a factory worker, beaming at the younger brother she had helped to educate. In a front room Coloured girls danced dreamily to the "Tennessee Waltz". Peter flitted between guests, chatted about Dylan Thomas and E. M. Forster, holding forth about the suffering of the Africans as if he were just another European journalist discussing an alien race; yet underneath feeling deeply the tragedy of his people, and thinking of his plane next day to Nairobi.

"The great thing about Africa," said Peter just before he left, "is what it teaches you about yourself. . . ."

CHAPTER FIVE

Back o' the Moon

Drum awarded a fifty-pound prize each year for the best African short story. The first winner was a young African teacher in Sophiatown, called Can Themba. "Watch that man Themba," wrote Peter Abrahams from London.

Can was a slender, bony man with a sensitive face, and a misleadingly innocent expression. He had a degree in English from Fort Hare, the African college in the Cape; and knew no African language. He combined a taste for Euripides and Blake with a restless life of intrigue and action in the streets and backyards of Sophiatown. We offered him a job. He said: "I'm it," and moved in.

Sophiatown was Can's life. He wrote about the thugs and liquor sellers and loose women with brisk detachment, catching the rough dialogue of Sophiatowners:

"The last bus to Sophiatown. About the eleven o'clock before midnight. Peter was waiting for the fish tin to rattle off. Then she came in.

" 'Hallo, Beautiful! Come sit with me,' someone called. Then a chorus of amateur wolves yelled, inviting her to come sit with them. And Peter noticed how she glanced round uneasily. She was looking for a safe seat near a gentleman. But he did not feel gallant. In Sophiatown you don't get gallant.

"Then he saw a thug coming up from the back to take her in hand. Suddenly she saw Peter and made up her mind.

" 'Hallo, Jerry!' she exclaimed, and went to sit by his side. Peter did not know her from Adam and Eve, and he felt sick.

The thug hesitated for a moment. Then he, too, decided. He was going to get tough.

"But she addressed herself to Peter again.

" 'When did you get out of gaol for murder, Jerry darling?' she cooed.

" 'Last week,' Peter muttered unhappily.

"The thug shuffled past to the door discreetly.

"Peter did not know whether his reputation had risen or fallen. But some girls do think fast, don't they?"

*　　　*　　　*

Can introduced me to Sophiatown. "Come to the Back o' the Moon," he said one evening. "It's a new shebeen I've just discovered. I think you'd be interested."

Shebeens are illegal African drinking places, where European liquor is sold at double prices. To the white man, Johannesburg is a city of cinemas, hotels, restaurants and night clubs. To the African, it is a city of shebeens. Can would point them out.

"You see those government offices there, with the passage down the side? Well, through that gate is Ma Dhlamini's. . . . You see this church, with steps beside? There's a shebeen there, they call it 'going to church'. . . . In the courtyard, up those stairs, is the Cabin in the Sky. . . . And just behind this office block, up the fire-escape is the Thirty-Nine Steps. . . . Then behind the post office is the House on Telegraph Hill. . . ."

But the most interesting shebeens were in Sophiatown. Can took me to the Back o' the Moon.

"It's my birfday," he explained, on the way.

"Birthday?"

"No, birfday. In Sophiatown, birthdays are too far apart. So we have birfdays once a month. . . ."

We drove off to "Berlin", a corner of Sophiatown, and parked in a small backyard. Can led the way through the darkness into a narrow passage beside a broken-down building. We squeezed past a man in a huge stetson and a fancy raincoat, enveloping a girl in the darkness. Can knocked briskly on a door, and shouted: "Fatsy!" through a crack. There was a noise of heavy feet, and two bolts were pulled; we walked into the lighted room.

"Hiya, Fatsy!" said Can, bowing at a vast woman with flesh bulging out everywhere like an eiderdown, whose face changed shape as she moved. She beamed at Can and me with a lazy smile; her comfortable face was infinitely friendly.

"Come in, fellers!" she said richly. "Make yourselves at home."

"Quite . . . quite . . ." said Can, manoeuvring round chairs. "By the way, Fatsy, let me introduce you. This is—er—Mr. Tony. Fatsy."

"How do you do?" I said.

"Very well, thank you, Mr. Tony," she said, in the African fashion. "And how do you?"

"Very well, thank you."

I looked round the bright room, blinking after the darkness. Beside a radiogram in the corner sat a middle-aged African woman with glasses, in a low-cut black dress, looking through a high pile of ten-inch records. Her hard brown face was covered with white powder, like flour on a stale doughnut, and her large lips were shiny with lipstick like blackberry jam. She gave Can a leer, and fluttered her long eyelashes. On a couch opposite, two men sat together, under broad-rimmed hats, clutching glasses of brandy and gazing silently at me.

We sat down in a corner, next to a man with a dark crinkled face, who peered at us through filmy eyes.

"Good evening, baasie!" he said suddenly, bobbing up and smiling fixedly as if I was taking his photograph.

"Hilda, give us some jive, man!" shouted Fatsy to the woman by the radiogram. "You see, we's got everything here, Mr. Tony! Open day and night! Every modern convenience. We do everything for customers. Don't we, Canny?"

57

"Quite, quite," said Can.

Hilda chose a record and walked mincingly to the radiogram. The jazz noise blared against the bare walls and rattled the loudspeaker. Fatsy, without warning, jumped into a jerky jive, shaking up and down like a jelly. She swayed in front of Can and me, with her podgy hands outstretched to an imaginary partner, while the floorboards creaked. Can shot up like a spring released, and jived wildly in front of her, and Fatsy shouted in delight.

Hilda joined in, with her dress slipping lower, and ogled the dark man next to me. He stood up gravely, as if to make a speech; then he performed a sedate jive, like compulsory P.T.

"Don't you jive, Mr. Tony?" shouted Fatsy. Everyone looked round at me, and I remembered I was white. "Don't be shy, Mr. Tony!" sang Fatsy to the rhythm, and lunged at Can and clasped him.

I walked over to the two men on the sofa, dodging the swinging bodies. They looked up at me, surprised but friendly.

"Do you know a paper called *Drum*?" I asked.

"Ya, baas, we know *Drum*. It's one of our African papers, baas!"

"Well, I'm the editor of the *Drum*."

"Aaaaah!" they said together. "So you're Mr. Drum, eh? Pleased to meet you, sir. My name's Patrick Mokwena, sir," one said, getting up and shaking hands.

"How do you do?"

"Very well, thank you, sir. How do you?"

"Very well, thank you."

"And my name's Selby Mhlangu," said the other.

"How do you do?"

"Very well, thank you, sir. How do you?"

"Very well, thank you."

I sat down with them.

"Soooooo! You're Mr. Drum!"

"My name's Tony, actually."

"Mr. Tony, eh? Did you take those snaps of Bethal, Mr. Tony? Say, those were it, man! Bethal! Gee, that's a place, eh! Gee, but the *Drum* boys get around the place! They know everything, man—each and everything, true's God!"

"Aaaaah! That *Drum*—it's got some dames in it. The guys are always saying, 'Gee, those *Drum* dames!'"

"Tell me, Mr. Tony, do you often come to Sophiatown? We're not used to white men in Sophiatown, you know! You're not South African?"

"No, English."

"Aaaaah! England, that's it. You come from London?"

"Yes."

"Gee, that's it! London's the place. No colour bar. That's where Jake Tuli is, in London, man! Have you met Jake Tuli, Mr. Tony? He's British Empire Flyweight Boxing Champion of the World—young Jake from Jo'burg! He's shown those white guys over there."

"It's true. He hits 'em like Moses. Our boxers are class, you know, Mr. Tony. If it wasn't for Mr. Donges, I tell you, they'd go over to England like flies. Like FLIES, man!"

Another man joined in.

"Hi, Wally, boy!" said Patrick.

"Hi, Paddy. Hi, Sel," said Wally sadly, with his hands deep in his raincoat pockets.

"Wally, this is Mr. Tony. He's one of the *Drum* boys, man."

Wally switched to a smile. "How do you do, baas?"

"Okay, baas!" I said, shaking hands.

Wally looked at me out of the corner of his eye, and threw his head back in laughter.

"Okay, Mr. Tony!" he said, and sat down beside us, looking gloomily out from his deep-set eyes.

"How's the woman?" said Patrick softly.

"Gone, man." Wally looked blankly up at Patrick.

"Martha's gone?"

"It's true. Last night. Takes everything. Furniture. Clothes. Curtains. Only leaves me with my books. She doesn't like books," he added sourly.

"Hell, Wally, boy; there's a thing," said Patrick.

"Aaaaah," said Selby.

"What do the boys say, Wally?" said Patrick. "What do the esquires say?"

"The esquires! They take the side of the woman, man."

"Hell, Wally, boy; I'm sorry. I'm real sorry. True's God. The esquires—your friends!"

"True to speak, they are not real friends," said Wally slowly, as though the words had rung in his mind all day. "But it's all in life."

"But these sheilas, they're all the same," said Patrick.

"Brother, I tell you, our African women are paid too muuuuch!" said Selby suddenly and fiercely. "The white man, he pays her seven pounds, and you four pounds.[1] What can you do? She can do what she likes. Each and every week they buy nylons, that's how much?"

"Twelve and six, brother," said Wally, automatically and grimly.

"And then they want cork-soled shoes—that's how much?"

"Eeeeee!" said Wally, as if he had been pricked. "Forty-five shillings, that's it."

"Then they want a new handbag. That's how much?"

"It's three guineas, brother."

"And then they want a hat that's just entirely the same as the old one, but with the flowers *just two inches farther back*," he said in a high-pitched voice. "That's how much?"

"It's two guineas."

"And the next week, she wants it two inches farther back

[1] Under the Industrial Conciliation Act, African women, but not men, are allowed to join trade unions, and hence are often able to earn much higher wages than their husbands.

again, and that's two guineas again. And then you say, No. And
so she says, 'It's my money, man.' So you say, No, again. So she
gets up and goes with all the furniture and bedclothes and
curtains. . . ."

"Aaaaah," says Wally. "And supposing, by the way, that
you get a woman from the kraals?"

"Brother, that's worse," said Selby, stamping on the table.
"When you find her, she's just wearing her skins. And then she
comes up to Jo'burg and sees all the motor cars and skyscrapers
and all the other sheilas and then she says: 'Man! I can't go
out like this. My dear, I must have one of those skirts, and
those stockings, and those hats. Please, my dear, my dear!' And
on. . . . and on. . . . Man, she wants to be modernised, that's the
trouble."

"She wants to be modernised," said Patrick. "It's true! It's
no good! So they get divorced like flies, like FLIES, man. And
then you have to get another sheila, and she's worse. Man,
they're all the same nowadays, true's God!"

From where I sat I could see through the screen in the corner
of the room. A large man with a dropped walrus moustache lay
on the double bed, in a dark suit; he had just woken up, and was
staring contentedly at a crumbling ceiling.

I rose and excused myself from Patrick and Selby.

"Can you put my snap in the *Drum*, Mr. Tony?" said Patrick,
fumbling with his wallet, and producing a crumpled brown
picture of himself concealed under a sisal hat, standing with his
arm round a glum girl, against a brick wall.

"I'm afraid we can only use a special kind of photograph."

"See you some more, Mr. Tony."

The man behind the screen emerged uncertainly; he noticed
me and blinked. He tottered in my direction. Can came quickly
up, extracting himself from Fatsy.

"Hiya, Dad! How's tricks? Can I introduce you to Mr.
Tony?"

"How do you do?" he said, grabbing my white hand in his thick black hand.

"Dad's a politician, Tony," said Can. "He's a Congress man, aren't you, Dad?" Can put his arm lightly round Dad's shoulder, and Dad grunted.

"I'm the boss of this joint," said Dad abruptly, looking furtively towards Fatsy. "I'm the boss here."

"A very nice place it is, too."

"So you're a white man," said Dad.

"Yes, I'm a friend of Can's."

"You're welcome here—very welcome. Make yourself at home, sir." He collapsed into a chair.

"What's Congress doing these days, sir?" I asked. Fatsy came up to Dad with a glass and a quarter-bottle of brandy; she muttered "Here!" sharply, and went away. Dad poured out some brandy, said, "Afrika!" and gulped it down. "Congress!" he shouted suddenly, and paused. "Up to maggots!"

"Don't you belong to Congress, then?"

"Ya. The African people must have their freedom—if you understand, sir. We want freedom from oppression—freedom from want—freedom from fear. Freedom! You understand, sir?"

"So you support Congress policy?"

"Up to maggots, man! What do they do? Tell me. Tell me. What do they do? What do they do?"

"I don't know."

"Nothing, man! What do the big bosses in Congress say? They say, 'We must fight to the last ditch. Resist! Go to jail!' And what do the bosses do? Nothing! Nix! Zero! And they want *us* to fight! Up to maggots, man!"

"Do you think that Congress leaders should defy the government?"

"It's true!" he said, looking at me approvingly. "They must fight, man! They're scared . . . that's what it is. They're *scared*!"

There was a sudden banging on the outside door, drowning every other noise. Instinctively, everyone drained their glasses. Fatsy, to my surprise, walked calmly to the door, and opened the bolts. The door was pushed open, and a man appeared in his shirt-sleeves, with half his shirt covered in blood, holding one arm over a wound on his shoulder. He rushed through into the adjoining room, muttering, "Gangsters. . . ." and disappeared. Fatsy bolted the door, and everyone began talking again, as if nothing had happened. Fatsy swayed up.

"You're coming to my Nice Time Party, Mr. Tony, aren't you?"

"What party?"

She rummaged in her dress and came out with a small yellow card, with a gold-deckled edge. "I'm expecting you, Mr. Tony," she giggled. "It's all weekend!" She wobbled off.

I looked at the card, printed in different type for each line.

HALLO! HALLO!! HALLO!!!
A GRAND NICE TIME PARTY
will be given by
ESMERELDA PHAKANE, known as FATSY
at Number 153, Gerty St. Sophiatown
On Friday 1st, Sat 2nd, Sun 3rd April 1952
Plenty Stag Foam and Juice, come and enjoy.
Admission 6/-
BUZ BUZ PRINTING WORKS

Jazz shrieked out again. Fatsy swerved towards Can, and snatched him up. Can's lean figure was almost surrounded by shaking flesh.

The record ended, and Fatsy ran to the radiogram. Can hopped nimbly across to me, whispered, "Quick! Let's get off," and made for the door. As we unfastened the bolt, Fatsy shouted across the room:

"Canny, boy! Where youse going?"

"It's okay, Fatsy. We're just getting something from Mr. Tony's car."

We went out into the dark. The embracing couple were still in the passage. As we splashed through the yard, I said:

"What's wrong? Police?"

"No, Fatsy. Kinda possessive."

We bumped into Dad, looking anxiously out into the street, his paunch pushed out before him.

"Youse leaving us, Mr. Tony, sir? See you some more. Always open. Night and day. It's my joint, you know. I'm the boss *there*. Always welcome at Back o' the Moon."

"Quite, quite," said Can, hopping impatiently.

"Youse got to be careful in Sof'town, sir. Big gangsters. Americans. Koreans. Berliners."

"Well, good night, sir."

"Good night, baas!" he said, bowing.

We slipped away to the car. As we slammed the doors, there was a deep guffaw from the back seat, and the car shook.

"Fatsy!" shrieked Can, and collected himself. "You want a lift somewhere?"

"Sure," crackled Fatsy.

"Where?"

"Where youse going, Canny?"

"I'm not going anywhere. I'm staying here, sis."

Can whispered: "Okay. See you at forty-six," and stepped out of the car.

"Goodbye, Tony!" Fatsy heaved herself out of the car, panting. "You'll come to my Nice Times, Mr. Tony?" she shouted, as I drove off.

I stopped outside No. 46. Can suddenly appeared, panting, and rushed into the car. I drove off.

"Near thing," said Can.

"The old boy seemed friendly," I said.

"Huh. He was waiting for you to get away. He's got a big burglary job tonight. He thought you might be a dick."

*   *   *

One evening, in a noisy Sophiatown shebeen, I watched a faithless husband hiding under the table from his wife, while his friends chased his mistress out of the window. "Big bioscope," said a fat man, shaking beside me. It came to me suddenly that I was watching an Elizabethan play. It was as if the characters had tripped straight from the stage of the Globe, lugging their dead bodies with them.

Sophiatown had all the exuberant youth of Shakespeare's London. It was the same upstart slum, with people coming from a primitive country life to the tawdry sophistication of the city's fringes. Death and the police state were round the corner; and there was the imminent stage direction:

Exeunt with bodies. . . .

CHAPTER SIX

Two Worlds

I stood on a smooth brown lawn, in the dry winter air of Johannesburg, sipping gin and tonic and scooping up cream cheese with potato crisps. People were talking gaily. Black servants in dazzling white suits, white shoes, white gloves, with red bandoleers across their chests, walked softly between the guests, offering drinks and savouries. The garden stretched down to a swimming-pool and a tennis court. The clear blue sky was unbroken by clouds.

Everybody was friendly. People had told me that white South Africans, underneath, were uneasy and afraid; but I could see no sign of it—they seemed happy and confident.

"So you've just come out from England?" asked the girl next to me.

"Well, nine months ago."

"What were you doing over there?"

"I was working with a printing firm. I'd just left Oxford. . . ."

"Oh, really? How interesting. I had a cousin at Oxford. What are you doing out here, then?"

"I'm a . . . sort of journalist."

"Which paper?"

"I don't suppose you know it. It's a magazine for Africans"—I could never avoid saying the word self-consciously, knowing that it stamped me at once as a "liberal"—"it's called *Drum*."

"Oh."

I waited for that "Oh". I could see her giving me an odd look, wondering what kind of a crank I was. I could see her mind working, because that was how my own mind worked, when I met a crank.

"Isn't *Drum* the one that had that Bethal article in it?"

"That's right."

"We used to take *Drum* for our native boys. But it seems to have changed a lot now. Wasn't Bob Crisp the editor?"

"Yes, I took over from him."

"Oh. I see." (Pause.) "I suppose the natives liked that Bethal article, didn't they?"

So it went on. I saw myself gradually forced into a role. I could never explain that *Drum* was a job, and our readers were human like anyone else. I saw white people eyeing me as a crank; and I began to feel a crank. Probably I ostracised myself more than they ostracised me. In white society, I began to feel a light chip on my shoulder.

As I penetrated farther into the world of Africans, I found myself caught between the two camps of black and white. The contrast, from a cocktail party in the northern white suburbs to a drinking den in the southern black locations, was abrupt.

"Shucks, Tony, what's wrong with you whites, man?" said Todd. "Gee! All this umming and erring. 'Ah, perhaps you wouldn't mind ah sitting ah here, Mr. Matshikiza.' " And Todd would tighten his mouth and clasp his hand in mimicry of a white host. " 'I ah suppose you don't ah hear very much ah classical music in ah Orlando, Mr. Matshikiza?' All this Mr. and would you mind! With us darkies, you're either welcome or you're not. If you're not, we chuck you out, just like that!" Todd kicked up his leg. "If you're welcome, you come in and stay, and *enjoy* yourselves, man! *We* don't stand around like a lot of statues. 'Would you ah pass another gin and ah lime, please.' " Todd stood stiffly, grinning inanely.

The contrast was stimulating. I saw one world in terms of the other, always slightly aloof: black against white and white against black.

There was an odd relationship between the two worlds. African beauty queens or fashionable hostesses in Orlando in the evening became kitchen girls in the white suburbs next morning. Masters of ceremonies and band leaders became waiters and "boys".

"Have you ever met the assistant editor of——?" I asked Henry.

"I haven't exactly *met* him," said Henry; "but of course I know a lot about him, because his cook was a girl-friend of mine, and I used to stay in the servants' room at the bottom of his garden."

Todd came to lunch one day at my flat; he was amazed by its size and its quietness.

"Gee, I don't think I could *live* here, Tony! It's so quiet. What does everyone *do*? Are they ill? Or dead? It isn't natural, man." He laughed, and listened to the silence.

As we sat down to lunch, the door bell rang and an African delivery boy came in to collect some empty bottles. Seeing Todd sitting down at the table, he laughed and winked, and gabbled something in Xhosa. As he was leaving, he picked up a bottle with some whisky left in it, which I had thought was empty; he looked up at me, and I took the bottle and put it away. After he had left, Todd said:

"Shucks, did you understand what he said to me? . . . He said: 'So! You're eating with an Englishman, are you? You're doing pretty well!' "

"Why did he say 'Englishman'?" I asked.

"Well, you see, he really means 'the sort of white man that might be eating with an African'. It couldn't be an Afrikaner, you see. Hell! And then did you notice when he picked up that bit of scotch?"

"Yes, why?"

"Well, that just shows how his mind was working. He thought: 'Shucks, if this guy eats with darkies, he'll probably

68

give me a spot!' But he was wrong! Hell, but these guys are pretty quick, you know! You have to watch out."

* * *

Cutting like a sharp knife between my two lives was the law of apartheid. At every turning were the signs SLEGS VIR BLANKES, NIE BLANKES, sorting the two races like an infallible machine, and sending them separate ways.

I could never forget about apartheid: it cut across nearly everything I tried to do. It made the job of white editor of a black paper awkward. I could never travel with Henry or Todd in the same train, taxi, bus or lift. We could not be together in a restaurant, a bar, a theatre or a park.

If Henry and Jurgen went on an assignment, they had to take two taxis, one white, one black. If they went to the station to take photographs, one entered by SLEGS VIR BLANKES, the other by NIE BLANKES. If I was travelling with Todd, and we wanted a meal, I walked into a restaurant, and Todd went "round the back" to the kitchen, where the "boys" were fed.

Even in the contents of the magazine, apartheid intervened. We were ticked off for showing a picture of Eleanor Roosevelt shaking hands with Mrs. Edith Sampson, a negro woman. We could not print photographs of a black boxer pummelling a white boxer. (Mixed boxing was forbidden in South Africa, and photographs of mixed fights were frequently held up by the South Africans, as constituting "incitement".)

I walked down to Orlando station one afternoon after seeing Henry, and took the first train back to Johannesburg. The compartment was full of Africans, and I listened to the conversation about white bosses. An Afrikaans ticket collector came in, and saw me.

"Why aren't you in the luggage-van?"

"I prefer it here."

"In that case you'll blerry well get out at the next station.

This is a native train, man. You can't travel on *this* train. . . ."

Jurgen was always having trouble. One day he arranged to take pictures of Dolly Rathebe, a famous African film star. He drove off with her in the office car, with a pile of dresses in the back, to the top of a goldmine dump outside Johannesburg, whose sandy top looked like a beach. On the way, Jurgen noticed a car following him. After he had taken a few photographs of Dolly reclining on the mine dump in a bathing costume, a car drew up and two policemen approached him.

"What are you doing here?"

"I'm taking photographs for a magazine."

They looked at Dolly in her scanty costume, and then at the pile of dresses inside the car. They arrested them both, and questioned them at the police station for two hours, suspecting them of illicit relations. Jurgen overheard one Afrikaans policeman saying:

"These Germans, you see; they come out to South Africa, and we think they're going to be good Nationalists, man. And what do they do? They go around with Kaffir girls . . ."

Johannesburg is split in two by apartheid. In the huge locations to the south, the black men spend their lives going to work, giving parties, marrying, having children, talking and playing. In the northern suburbs, the white men spend their lives, too, going to work, giving parties, marrying, having children. Like a shuttle, the two races come together every day to do their work together, and at night they automatically separate and retreat their different ways. One half never knows what happens to the other half.

That is the great secret. The protection of this secret is the sacred duty of apartheid. By the elaborate and costly system of separate entrances, areas, trains, buses, trams, cinemas, telephone boxes, lifts, lavatories, waiting rooms—not to mention God's gift of separate skins—people forget the obvious—that both halves are human, and essentially their lives are the same.

Apartheid had become a belief so strong that it superseded all other human and moral values.

"You know, Toddy, I saw a white woman fall down in the street yesterday," said Henry one morning. "I was just going up to help her, and then I stopped, and thought: What will the whites think? They'll think I'm trying to rape her. If I pick her up, it means I'll actually have to touch her. A native touching a European woman! Oooh! Terrible! I couldn't risk it, so I walked on. . . ."

"Surely, in a case like that——" I said.

"Of course the whites would think that," said Todd. "It's always happening, isn't it, Hen? A doctor friend of mine was driving to Durban. He comes across a car smash, with some whites badly hurt. So the doc takes off his coat to keep them warm, and makes some bandages. Then some whites come along in a car. 'What are all these natives doing here?' they say. That's true, Hen, isn't it? So they shoo the doc away. 'Next time I'll let 'em die,' he said. Didn't mean it, of course. But shucks! 'What are all these natives doing here?'"

Two weeks later, I heard Alan Paton, the author of *Cry the Beloved Country*, speaking at a meeting:

"Who is there here who would not hesitate to come to the aid of an African woman who stumbled in the street? And if you say that no one would hesitate, I must tell you that there is at least one, and he is speaking to you on this platform—now."

*   *   *

Todd Matshikiza, more than any other of our staff, was a man of two worlds. With his genius for friendship, and his musical talents, he moved easily among Europeans. Yet, unlike most urban Africans, he had never rejected his tribal roots, and took pride in them.

Todd's grandfather was a famous witch doctor near Queenstown, in the Xhosa district of the Cape; he was expert at the

71

wriggling dance used by witch doctors to find out evil spirits, and they gave him the name of Tshikiza, to shake. Todd's father was a civil servant, and a well-known musician. The family kept some of their faith in magic. When Todd was at school, the local witch doctor smeared crosses on the bottom of his gym shoes with pork fat, so that he should win the music competitions. He won.

Todd was brought up in Queenstown, a small English-speaking country town where the colour bar was not strict. When he was six, he made friends with Donald, a white boy of his own age; they spent all their time together, and lived in each other's houses. When Donald was given a bicycle by his father, Todd was given a bicycle. When Todd got a trumpet, Donald got a trumpet. When he was eleven, Donald went away to boarding school, and Todd saw him off at the station.

A year later, Todd saw Donald at the other side of the street; he shouted over to him. Donald looked round, stared at him, and looked away. They never spoke to each other again.

When he grew older, Todd was employed by a Queenstown café to play the piano for the white customers. He could see African faces pressed against the window outside, gazing at the black man among the white people.

During the war, the R.A.F. opened a camp outside Queenstown, and the British airmen came to listen to Todd playing at the café; they invited him back to the camp, and he found himself suddenly away from the barrier of colour.

But Todd began to feel more sharply the pain of the colour bar. One day he noticed that Bach's *St. Matthew Passion* was being performed at a church nearby; he went to the vicar, and asked him if Africans were allowed to listen.

"My friend, you know there is no colour bar in the Anglican Church," said the vicar.

"But you always have the separate churches for Africans and Europeans," said Todd.

"Ah, but that is just for convenience; of course you are welcome to come along to our church."

Todd went, and was ushered to a seat at the back, behind a pillar. The church was nearly empty. He never went again.

When he was twenty, in the holidays from Lovedale College, he underwent the Xhosa initiation ceremony. "Say 'I am a man,'" said the *Ingcibi*, or tribal surgeon, after the painful circumcision. "Ndiyi Ndoda—I am a man."

Then Todd was taken to a small hut in the garden, and smeared his body all over with white chalk. For seven days he was not allowed to drink water, or to eat anything except dried maize. He could not leave the hut except at nights; if he saw a woman, he had to squat on the ground, and cover himself with his blanket.

He lay alone in the hut, sleeping with only an old blanket on the hard floor. He could hear his brother playing Duke Ellington in the house. "It was a wonderful time," said Todd. "I felt completely at peace."

After three weeks, Todd was taken down to the river, and the white chalk was washed off; he was handed a new set of clothes, and all his old ones were given away. For another two months, he was forbidden to talk to any woman, even his mother, except through an intermediary.

On the last day, the chief came for the great ceremony of manhood. Two sheep were slaughtered, and all Todd's relations gathered round. "You are now welcome into the society of men," said the chief. "You are now your father's father."

"It gave me a sense of confidence and responsibility, which I would never otherwise have had," said Todd. "I would like my children to have it, too."

Todd slipped easily from one world to another. He felt and showed no strain between his Xhosa tribal background and his European way of life. "I've had a happy life," he said.

"There have been moments of bitterness. But apartheid makes things difficult now. I'd hate my children to have less than me."

Todd invited me to dinner one evening at his house in Orlando, with a white friend, Roger. We drove through pitch-dark Orlando, past rows of identical brick box houses, till we found Todd's little white semi-detached house, No. 8385B, Orlando.

Todd came out to welcome us. He took us into the brightly-lit room, with gay curtains, a bright yellow screen, carpeted floor, and books and records everywhere. The dinner table was laid for seven. Todd's wife, Esmé, Arthur and two friends were waiting. We talked, and the bareness and sordidness of the location outside were forgotten.

Roger asked Todd about Orlando.

"The municipality call this part Dingiswayo—that's after one of our chiefs; but we all call it Killarney, after the posh white suburb. Darkies are great snobs, you know!"

Todd played a recording of "Hamba Kahle" ("Go Well," the African "goodbye"), the choral song which he had composed for the Queen Mother at Bulawayo. He poured out some Spanish sherry. We sat down to table, and Esmé served roast beef and Yorkshire pudding. We talked about writing, and who would be the first of us to write a book.

"Shucks, Tony, there's so much I could write about. Whites, for instance: there's a lot I'd like to write about whites. Like the other day, when I was walking down Eloff Street with Scarpe, and two white girls behind us said: 'Listen to those natives! They're talking English! Hee hee!' But the trouble is, Tony, I can't write about these things without getting angry. I prefer to forget them. Anyway, what I really want to do is to compose. Music's the thing, man! . . ."

The conversation was drowned by a noise of tramping boots and shouting at the door, which had been left open. I noticed

74

Arthur's face go tense, and Todd's words died. Six African policemen were standing in the doorway.

The sergeant went up to the table and grabbed the bottle of sherry.

"Now we've caught them!" he said. "Now we've got the clever doctors and teachers who have white men to their houses. This will show them how clever they are."

"That bottle is mine. It's not his fault. . . ." But Roger faded out as he watched Todd shaking his head furiously. (Supplying liquor to natives is a much worse offence than possessing it.)

Todd looked about helplessly, while the sergeant and his gang searched the cupboards for more liquor. They went through to the bedroom.

"They're worse than the whites!" muttered Todd. "They'll do anything to please their white baas. That sergeant will expect promotion for this. . . ."

"Why did they come here?"

"The neighbours must have told them; they probably saw white people come in, and were jealous. . . ."

The police trudged back. The sergeant roughly told Todd and Arthur to follow him to the police station. He turned to me.

"And you, baas, please go to the police station, and see the baas there." We left the half-finished dinners on the table. Todd and Arthur walked off with the police, shrugging their shoulders.

Roger and I drove down to the police station. I wondered what we could be charged with. It was difficult to know in Orlando when one was breaking the law. We waited at the police station while Arthur and Todd queued to pay their fines: five pounds for Todd, for possessing liquor, and one pound for Arthur, for being in Orlando without a permit. Todd overheard two of the African constables who had arrested us talking in Zulu.

"You know what, man? We should have taken the white

75

baasies with us and beaten them up, and taken their money. They were rich, man!"

We wandered round the building, watching drunks being dragged in, and the people waiting to pay fines, with expressionless faces and tired eyes. After two hours, an Afrikaans sergeant arrived and called us into his office, with a look of disgust.

"What are you doing in this location?"

"I'm a journalist. I'm writing about Orlando."

"You got a permit to be in Orlando?"

"No, but this is part of my job. . . ."

"Doesn't matter. If you've got no permit, I must make a charge." He brought out a form and a pen, and took my name and address slowly, looking up at me with a mystified expression.

"And where was you arrested?"

"Just up the road. I was having supper with a native friend of mine. . . ." He looked up at me in horror.

"Sis, man! You tell me you was actually sitting down eating with a native? . . ."

"Yes."

"Eating with a native! Hell, man, I was thinking of letting you go just now. But now I've got half a mind to put you straight in the cells!" He could hardly bring himself to look at me. "Can't you see the troubles you're making? Any moment now, and all the blerry natives in Orlando will want to sit down with Europeans. How can you do it, man? Eating with natives. . . . Ag, it makes me sick, man." And he really looked sick.

At all costs we had to avoid more trouble.

"Ag," growled the sergeant, chewing his pen, "I don't know what you want to do it for, man!" He seemed genuinely hurt. He looked up and down from his form, giving me quick, puzzled glances.

"Ag, man, go away! Get out of Orlando. If I catch you here again, I'll have you flogged."

CHAPTER SEVEN

Live Fast, Die Young

When we decided to write about crime in *Drum*, there was no lack of material. Crime was not, as in Britain, a vicarious excitement for suburban lives: it was a day-to-day reality for nearly all our readers. Their survival depended on keeping on the right side of gangsters. Black Johannesburg is largely ruled by criminals: they have the big money, the big cars, the best girls. If you offend them, they will beat you up. If you bring a case against them, they will beat up the witnesses. If you cause them any further trouble they will kill you. At the inquest, the witnesses will be absent.

Johannesburg has one of the highest crime rates in the world. One in thirty of the Africans on the Reef can expect to be murdered in the course of his lifetime. Every other African will have been assaulted sufficiently seriously to reach the police. Four hundred and forty-seven Africans were murdered on the Reef in 1950, out of a total non-European population of just under a million; about the same number were (officially) raped. Among those million people there are two murders a day: in Britain, with fifty million, there is a murder every two days.

"I suppose you wouldn't think, Mr. Sampson, that I'd murdered two men?" said Les, a well-dressed young Coloured sitting with me at the Cosy Café, near the law courts. To prove his point, he fished out of his pocket a small black automatic.

"I've been a gangster since I was fifteen. I went to the

bioscope, and thought it would be exciting and big to have my own gun. But, gee, I'd do anything to get out of it now. It's hell. I can't trust anyone, you know. I daren't quit—they wouldn't let me. They'd think I'd squeal on them. I've *got* to go on. . . ."

He looked up at me melodramatically. He'd picked up that dialogue, I imagined, at the latest bang-bang films. But soon after, I heard that Les *had* gone straight, and was working as a carpenter. A few months later, he was back in crime.

It was easy to talk to killers and thieves at the Cosy Café, above the noise of the juke-box and the ping of the pin-table. They loved talking about the crimes they had committed, and the stories they told were true.

The barrier of apartheid protected gangsters against the law: white police could never penetrate the black underworld, and were more concerned with passes and permits than with black men murdering each other. The black cities of Orlando or Alexandra were a gangster's paradise. The police tended to regard all blacks as equally savage. Any of our staff were as likely to go to jail for not carrying a pass as a gangster was. The white man's classification of all black men as alike was as convenient for the gangsters as it was inconvenient for respectable citizens.

It was never easy, in any case, to distinguish criminals from honest men. The first crime article we published in *Drum* was about the *tsotsis*. They are young small-time criminals who often have respectable jobs during the day, and supplement their earnings with handbag snatching, shoplifting, housebreaking or robbery by assault, at nights or at weekends.

"Can you find someone to pose as a *tsotsi* for a picture?" I asked Henry.

"Yes, of course," said Henry, who could always produce anyone; he came back with a gay young dandy.

"Mr. Sampson, let me introduce you to Spike; he plays the sax in a band, and works as a clerk in town. He's agreed to dress up as a *tsotsi* for us."

Spike was wearing the *tsotsi* rig, with very narrow "sixteen-bottom" trousers, a long floppy coat, a bright scarf tucked into it, and a slouch hat. He smiled broadly. After Spike had left, I said to Henry:

"He certainly acted the part very well."

"He wasn't acting." Henry shook with laughter. "You don't think he could live as well as that if he wasn't a *tsotsi*?"

I met several *tsotsis* like Spike; many were intelligent and well educated, with good jobs. They were open and friendly and soon talked openly about their second profession. "What's your brother doing now?" "Oh, at the moment he's a *tsotsi*."

To some extent the *tsotsis* were the African aristocracy. They not only earned more money, and led a more comfortable life, but they were often in the first place more lively and intelligent than their law-abiding brothers. "American scientists have proved that gangsters have low intelligence," we wrote in *Drum*; but I had my doubts.

The legal opportunities for an ambitious young African were small, and the rewards of crime were big. You could land up in jail for lack of a pass; and to be called a "criminal" was no great insult. Many *tsotsi*, after a few years of housebreaking or shoplifting, retired quietly from crime, with enough money to marry and have children.

Chatting with gangsters at the Cosy Café, I grew to understand the pressure towards crime. On top of the usual factors which make a juvenile delinquent was the eternal humiliation of black life in a white city—the constant rejection and exclusion. Gangster films, street-corner gambling, drinking to get drunk, were open to all. Theatres, decent houses, open spaces, libraries, travel abroad, were for Europeans only.

A good-looking African called Bill came often to the office, and helped with odd jobs. He was seventeen, shy and with perfect manners. He dressed immaculately, without being flashy. "Such a nice, polite native," said Europeans.

One morning, in the office, there was a loud bang from the direction of Henry's desk. Henry jumped up, and turned to see a little round hole in the wall behind him. On the opposite wall was a .22 bullet.

We rushed to the dark-room, where the bullet had come from. Inside was Bill, holding a primitive-looking automatic, and looking puzzled. "I was only cleaning it," he said.

Later, I knew Bill well. He lived in a slum corner of Johannesburg, and his mother was a shebeen queen. His boyhood hero was "the Sheik", an Indian gangster living nearby, who ruled the Johannesburg underworld.

Bill was attracted to crime not for money, but for excitement. When some money disappeared from the petty cash, we suspected wrongly that Bill might have taken it. He was very hurt. "I could have done a bank robbery, perhaps—but not two pounds from *Drum*."

Bill's favourite book was *Knock on Any Door*, by an American negro, Willard Motley, which described the downfall of a young gangster, "Pretty Boy". "Live fast, die young, and have a good-looking corpse," was Pretty Boy's motto. It was Bill's motto too.

After the gun incident, we thought that Bill had finished with shooting. But one morning I had a phone call to say that Bill had been arrested on a charge of attempted murder. I went to Marshall Square police station, and found Bill waiting calmly in his cell.

"I've managed to get some fags smuggled in," he said cheerfully. "The warders are okay; I call them baasie, and they're happy."

He seemed to enjoy the drama of arrest. He had shot at a girl while he was drunk in a shebeen. But he was still a juvenile, and he escaped with a fine; after that, I think he saw himself as "the man they couldn't catch".

Bill was always talking about gangster films.

"Jeez, have you never seen *Street with No Name?*" he said to me.

"You ought to see that, Tony," said Can; "you won't understand our readers until you've seen Stiles."

We did not need to wait long before *Street with No Name* came back to the local non-European cinema. I went with Can, Bill and Johnny.

The cinema was packed with *tsotsis*, shouting and cat-calling. I was the only white man. As I sat down, between Bill and Can, I heard a murmur behind me of "Laanis", the *tsotsi* word for white men. Everyone was talking Afrikaans, *tsotsi* slang or Chicago-ese. A man in a straw boater and a green and yellow open shirt turned round to us from the next row, snarling as he chewed gum. "Say, ain't youse the *Drum* guys, brother?"

The lights dimmed, and the film began, with a sequence showing the F.B.I. at work, and a personal message from Edgar Hoover, F.B.I. chief, to say that crime does not pay. A tough police detective was preparing to smash a gang of killers. The *tsotsis* went on talking and shouting and cuddling their girlfriends in the dark. Occasionally they jeered at the F.B.I.

The scene shifted to the gangsters' hideout. A hush from the audience. Richard Widmark appeared in one corner. A shriek from the whole house. "Stiles! Attaboy! Go it, Stiles!" A tense silence.

Stiles wore a long overcoat, sniffed a Benzedrine inhaler, and occasionally bit an apple. Beside him slouched his henchman, wearing a belted raincoat with slits at the back.

"When this film first came out," Can whispered, "the sales of Benzedrine rocketed. Everybody munched apples. All the *tsotsis* wore those raincoats."

81

"There's only one guy who's the brains of this outfit, and that's me," said Stiles. He planned the next robbery with a map. "When he comes out, you go there. See? And you go that end. Understand? Remember, till I say, no shooting."

The audience fidgeted with excitement, relaxing only when the F.B.I. appeared again. The film ended with a chase. A short gangster threw a knife at a night watchman, who dropped on the floor. "Kort boy!" shouted someone behind us.

"Did you hear that?" whispered Can. "Kort boy's a big gangster on the Reef, who throws a knife just like that. . . . He's doing eighteen years for murder."

Stiles was shot dead by the F.B.I. The audience groaned, as the F.B.I. took over. The *tsotsis* trooped out of the cinema, and gathered outside. Bill pointed out his gangster friends.

"There's Scarface. . . . There's Durango Kid. . . . Hiya, Jungle! Mr. Sampson, this is Jungle—he's head of the Thousand-and-One. Jungle, this is the editor of *Drum*."

"Say, you're Mr. Drum, eh? Say, why did ya write all that bull about the Thousand-and-One doing that Pretoria kidnap job, eh?"

"Well, wasn't it you?"

"Bull! That wasn't my boys; Thousand-and-One don't play around with kidnap. You shouldn't write that bull, man."

Driving back to Sophiatown, Bill and Johnny recited the dialogue of the film.

"That's was a sweet job you pulled in Pittsburg. . . ."

"No conviction! . . ."

"And that nice little shooting match in Miami. . . ."

"No conviction! . . ."

"And that surprising incident in Chicago. . . ."

"No conviction! . . ."

"Remember, guys, I'm de brains of dis outfit. . . ."

Can turned to me.

"You know, I've seen *tsotsis* in Sophiatown planning petty

robberies as if they were Stiles and his gang: they draw a map, which nobody understands, and the 'brains of the outfit' tells them where to go. . . ."

Bill had a friend called Gray, who at twenty-two was already a big name in the underworld. He had a gang of his own, which terrorised the Coloured township of Coronationville. He belonged to the crime "syndicate" run by the Sheik. He had murdered two men.

"I've got a story for you," said Bill one morning. "Gray's been converted. He wants to write his story for *Drum*."

Gray came into the office; he had a gentle manner, and talked quietly.

"The thing is, Mr. Sampson, I want to write about my conversion in *Drum*, so that the other guys can hear about it. Brother Olson, he's the guy that converted me, thinks it's a good idea. I don't want any money."

Gray dictated his story to Arthur: how he had first joined a gang when he was thirteen; how the Sheik had offered him five hundred pounds to wipe out a rival, which he did; how he had been beaten up by his rivals and "been through the meat-grinder"; how one day he found a note from Brother Olson, pinned to the inside of his door, and joined Brother Olson's open-air hymn-singing meetings.

"You ought to meet Brother Olson—he's a terrific guy," said Gray. "He's an American missionary; he and his pals converted the gangsters in Chicago. He's really tough!"

Gray brought Brother Olson round to the office. He was an impressive man, burly with bright blue eyes.

"Yes, I reckon our friend Gray has seen the light," he said. "But you can never be sure; it's kinda difficult to get these chaps a good job to keep them away from crime, you know. . . ."

We published Gray's *Confessions of an ex-Gangster* in five instalments. It was a success. "Dear Mr. Drum, thank you for publishing Gray's story. Now I can see that it is never too late to repent from crime. . . ." wrote one reader.

Gray seemed happy in his new life. He lived at home, looking after his grandmother, and worked as an upholsterer; he came often to the office, and tried to convert the staff. "The devil's pleasure is only for a season," he said, "whereas joy from God is everlasting." He left some verses on the evils of drunkenness on my desk.

Just after part three of Gray's story had appeared, Bill said: "I saw Gray with his old gang last night."

"For God's sake keep him straight," I said, thinking more of our articles than his soul. Gray came into the office next day.

"Those gangsters won't leave me alone, Mr. Sampson; they just think I'm being sissy."

Brother Olson pleaded with Gray, argued, warned and cajoled him; but Gray was slipping back.

"There's going to be trouble any day now," said Bill. We sent Gray down to Cape Town, where he had friends, with a single ticket. Two weeks later he was back, in a stolen car.

Just after the last instalment was published, Gray was sentenced to nine months' imprisonment for theft.

"Tell me, Mr. Drum, why do you say Gray has been converted, if he has just gone to jail?" wrote an observant reader. I met Brother Olson afterwards in a coffee bar.

"I'm afraid our friend Gray is powerfully confused," he said.

One of the gangsters Gray mentioned in his story sued us unsuccessfully; we could never tell whether gangsters would be infuriated or flattered by our exposures. Once, after discussion with our solicitors, we risked a libel action with an attack on an Indian gang. Three days after it appeared, we had a letter from the gang leader thanking us warmly for the publicity.

Checking through one article by Henry, I discovered a defamatory sentence about an African footballer being a gunman in his spare time.

"Why do you write this sort of thing?" I said testily. "Don't you know it'll get us into trouble?"

"By the way, I showed it to him first," said Henry. "He was very pleased with it."

More often, the gangsters bitterly resented our exposures and suspected that *Drum* was working with the police.

"Why don't we expose the Americans?" someone suggested at an editorial conference. The "Americans" were one of the most powerful of Johannesburg's *tsotsi* gangs, based on Sophiatown. No one seemed keen on exposing them.

"I like living," someone said from the back. "I stay next door to an American." There was a silence, and then Benson, a young reporter, said:

"Okay, sir, I'll write about the Americans."

The Americans were the "bosses" of Sophiatown. They took everything they wanted. When a teacher stopped an American from interfering with a schoolgirl, he was set on a few days later and beaten to death.

They wore expensive "American" clothes which gave them their name—straw hats, elegant cardigans, brown and white shoes and narrow blue trousers called "Bogarts" because Humphrey Bogart once wore them. They drove Buicks, and girls clustered round them.

During the working day, the Americans travelled to town in cloth caps and dustcoats, looking like any other African workers. In this disguise they stole clothes and materials from shops and railway sidings, often under the eyes of the white baas. They took them quickly off on a delivery bicycle, wearing their brown coats, safe in the anonymity of the black world.

When Benson brought me back his article, I gave it to Can, who lived in Sophiatown, to check the facts.

"That's fine; it's all correct," said Can. "I love the bit where Benson says 'the Americans are so well set up in Sophiatown that they employ the services of a B.A. to write their love letters.'"

"Why?" I asked. "Isn't it true?"

"It's true all right," he said. "I'm the B.A."

The Americans were called "the African Robin Hoods". "They rob the rich white men to pay the poor black men," said Africans. The gangs of thieves sold their stolen goods in the locations far cheaper than they could be bought in the shops.

"The *tsotsis* are a nuisance," an African teacher told me one evening; "but they have their uses. . . . I got my Parker 51 in the location for a pound—it costs six in the shops. I never bother to go to town for shopping these days; I find it's cheaper and easier in the location, *back door*."

"Back door" was big business. Thieves and shop-lifters, mainly sophisticated African girls, took suits, dresses, watches, pens, even typewriters and gramophones, from the smart white shops in town to the dingy hideouts in the locations, where they were sold at "African prices". I was having tea with some Africans in Moroka when a Plymouth drove up and a man brought in a pile of women's dresses; they each had the label with the shop price reduced to a third.

At the Back o' the Moon I overheard Peggy, a shop-lifter, talking to Boy, her boy-friend. She called herself, not a shop-lifter, but a "Noasisa" or "watcher". She never talked about stealing, but "taking". She had just left jail after a six months' sentence for "taking"; Peggy was a pretty, sophisticated girl, smartly dressed, with a well-cut coat and the "Noasisas" wide flared skirt, concealing stolen materials underneath. She asked about her friends.

"And Doris? Is she still working?"

"No, man! She's inside—six months."

"Poor Doris. It's tough, man. But it's worth it, in a biiig way. Gee, I love taking! Maisie and I work together now, in a big way. Not that prostitute business—walking up and down. No, man, that's wicked—selling your body, it's not right. But taking from the white shops, that's niiice—in a big way. Maisie knows all the tricks, man. And can she speak slang. Gee, I want to talk slang. Boy, teach me to talk slang, will you, man?"

Some Africans had little compunction about buying "back door". They regarded stealing from the whites rather as I remember some British officers regarded looting from the Germans.

Shopping "back door" had few dangers. Once the goods had disappeared into the black world, they were almost impossible to retrieve. "Back door" was the more expensive by-product of apartheid. The sharp division of black and white made all black crimes safer—blacks were unlikely to betray their own race, and whites dared not penetrate the black locations. Theft and prevention in an apartheid world build up into a vicious circle. Whites hire watchmen, keep guns, put up bars and burglar alarms, pay huge insurance premiums. By arming themselves against *tsotsis*, they often succeed in arming the *tsotsis*. A young *tsotsi* at Diepkloof Reformatory told us about his first robbery.

"I was looking for money, but could find none. But in one of the bedrooms, under a pillow, I found a baby Browning gun. This was better than money. . . ."

An African gangster can buy a gun "back door" at not much above the price in the shops—twelve pounds for a small automatic. The more guns that Europeans buy to protect their homes, the more find their way into the hands of the *tsotsis*.

*　　*　　*

Most sinister of the Johannesburg gangs were the "Russians". Unlike others, they were strongly tribal in origin; they were all Basutos, and had come from the poor, proud independence of Basutoland to the slum township of Newclare, near Sophiatown.

Their uniform symbolised their predicament; they wore expensive gaberdine trousers and smart hats; but in place of coats, they wore large blankets draped round them, defiant in their very design. A favourite pattern showed British fighter planes and bombs revolving round a crown, with "V" for Victoria, the great white Queen. The stately blanketed figures walked gravely up and down the slimy streets of Newclare, their tribal dignity still about them.

Between the Russians in Newclare and the neighbouring gang across the railway line, the "Civic Guards", there was deadly rivalry; each claimed they were protecting citizens against the other, and vied for control of the township. One evening, two Russians arriving home by train were set upon by Civic Guards at the railway station, and stabbed to death. Civil war broke out in Newclare between Russians and "Civics," which the railway line running between. A "Civic" schoolboy was murdered as he passed through Russian territory. A Russian in the "Civic" zone was hacked to death. In three days, ten people were murdered. Hundreds of armed police arrived in lorry loads, and patrolled the frightened streets.

I visited Newclare with Jurgen on the third evening of the war. We drove through the empty streets, with the shops boarded up and windows shuttered. Suddenly, round the corner, we found the road blocked by a group of Russians standing motionless in a circle, watching a Basuto war-dance in the moonlight. They were swathed in blankets up to their mouths, hats pulled low over their ears, intent eyes peering beneath. They carried a grotesque collection of weapons—long two-headed axes, shining two-foot knives, rusty daggers, clubs and knob-kerries. Inside the circle, frenzied war-dancers kicked, wriggled and shouted their war-cries, to the rhythm thumped from oil cans.

We watched this sudden apparition of the antique Africa uncovered in the midst of Johannesburg. The faces looming from the darkness bore no trace of the taming of the city—they were faces from the mountains and cliffs of Basutoland. Jurgen flashed his camera, while the spectators stared on—his picture contained a whole history of Africa.

Half an hour later, armed police swooped down, and confiscated all the weapons. Next day, the civil war was over, and the Russians reduced to impotence. Our glimpse of the wild life of Johannesburg had been only momentary.

*　　*　　*

These *tsotsi* gangs were all part of what we called the "Chaka complex". (Chaka was the founder of the Zulu nation, who massacred defeated tribes and ruled his regiments with iron discipline, until he was murdered by Dingaan in 1828.) During the war, Hitler was a kind of hero to the *tsotsis*; he reminded people of Chaka. They would call Hitler "Mkize", "u-Dhlamini", according to their tribe. Jungle, Dragon, Black Diamond, Gestapo, Berliners, Stonebreakers, Black Koreans, Spoilers. . . . The gangs' and gangsters' names told their own story.

Drum's relations with gangsters were uneasy. After we had published an exposure of the Sheik, Gonny Govender, our Indian reporter, complained that he was followed by a Buick full of the Sheik's thugs. We put a photograph of the Sheik in our display case, and an hour later it was torn down.

One morning I had a phone call.

"You's the editor?"

"Yes."

"My name's Solly. They say you're going to put me in the next *Drum*."

"I've never heard of you."

"Yes, you have. I'm the Sheik's brother. I'm telling you, mister, if you put me in *Drum* you'll look like you had six train accidents."

We put Solly, a petty housebreaker and thug, in the next *Drum*, but nothing happened. Whenever after that we touched a dangerous story, Henry would say:

"Do you want six train accidents?"

On my white eminence I was safe, but the African staff had to steer a dangerous course between *tsotsis* and police. "Why d'ya want to tell *die laanis* our tricks, man?" the *tsotsis* would complain.

We ran an article called "Clean up the Reef", challenging the police to eliminate danger spots like "Bullet Corner" and "Murder Street". The police took the challenge seriously, and the *tsotsis* were furious. One morning Henry, who had a hand in the article, was stopped by the police on his way to the office, and found without a pass. He was handcuffed and taken off to jail for the night. He found the jail full of *tsotsis* who had been picked up from the streets. He asked the Afrikaner warder what was happening.

"Ag, haven't you read the blerry *Drum*, man? We're cleaning up the Reef."

CHAPTER EIGHT

Dear Readers

Though *Drum*'s circulation was increasing, it was a tiny fraction of our potential readership of nine million Africans in South Africa, six million in Central Africa, and the hundred and fifty million in the whole continent.

It was this great illiterate, primitive mass that was our eventual target. How could *Drum* approach them? They were in the throes of a transition more abrupt and violent than any conquered people had faced before—from a primitive stone-age world of Africa to the complicated twentieth-century world of Europe. They had been uprooted from a slow rural existence and dumped in a fast-moving, sophisticated city.

How could we sell magazines to these confused and simple people?

We tried a circulation stunt; we published Henry's photograph, calling him "Mr. Drum", and let him loose in a location, promising five pounds to the first person, holding a copy of the paper, who found him.

I watched the hunt. It was not a success. The hot, dusty location seethed with people holding copies of *Drum*, following the car about, shouting "Mr. Drum" at me and Arthur in the back, misunderstanding the game in every possible way. They found two bogus Mr. Drums, tall and thin where Henry was stocky, and nearly lynched them in their anxiety to keep them. At last Henry persuaded someone to recognise him, and thankfully handed out the five pounds. But the angry crowd refused to accept Henry as the authentic Mr. Drum, and thought they had been tricked. Henry jumped into the car, and we nosed our way through a threatening mob.

I watched the people looking at *Drum*. There was one old Zulu whose face was lined like corrugated iron, with grey kinky hair, and loops of skin hanging from the lobes of his ears. He walked up to a boy with slow dignity, took up a copy of *Drum*, and stared at the advertisement on the back, upside down. After some time, he nodded his head gravely, smiled in a satisfied way, and gave it politely back.

I always remembered that old Zulu. What went on in his mind as he peered at the upside-down advertisement? What was *Drum* to him? How could we communicate with him across the centuries, or stir up anything but bewilderment in his mind? He was the simplest African that was our eventual target, the African African, untouched by the Western world.

Communication was our basic problem. Amusing and educating our readers was only secondary. First we had to establish some patch of common ground, some part of *Drum* which would be familiar and comprehensible to our simplest readers. We had to make *Drum* so that the old Zulu would pick it up and open it, and give that long comprehending "Aaaaah" which would mean that a bridge had been built between him and us.

We never quite built that bridge. The gulf was too wide. But slowly we came closer to that remote African, and heard faint signals of recognition. I began to guess why he would linger on page twenty-three, where there was an advertisement of a middle-aged woman polishing an oil lamp, and skip over page twenty-five, an astonishing scoop picture of two men fighting with daggers; why he preferred small, muzzy, out-of-focus snapshots of blank grey faces against brick walls, to vivid full-page three-colour illustrations of handsome couples in exciting situations; why he would thumb rapidly through articles about ritual murder or overcrowded trains, and suddenly stop at a small dim picture in a corner, showing a man in overalls holding a tyre, and say "Aaaaah!"

"*Drum*—me. Me—*Drum*." Identification. Recognition. Not other people, strange things. Just Me. Me in *Drum*. Ordinary Me. That, I think, was what "Aaaaah" meant.

I became enthralled by this problem of communication with the masses, through a magazine. We spent hours at conferences every month discussing reactions of readers and new ways of approaching them. Henry, Arthur, Todd and the others were, in many ways, as far removed from these people as I was: "mad with higher education", said a Basuto proverb. (I had, at least, a sentimental hankering for the peasant life which they lacked altogether.)

We discussed covers interminably; sometimes, after ten of us had looked at six covers in a row, casting our vote, I would say to Henry: "Fetch a clot." And Henry would go out and pick up a tattered Zulu from the street, and show him the six covers.

"You see these books? You've only got one sixpence, you see? Which book would you buy, eh?"

The Zulu paused, beamed and pointed to a picture hanging on the wall, of generals in the First World War, and said:

"That one, baasie!"

Drum had, at all costs, to be friendly and familiar, to combine excitement with ordinariness.

We spent hours watching people looking through *Drum*, noting the pictures they stopped at, and when they said "Aaaaah." A few subjects, which we varied endlessly, seemed to catch the African mind.

The African boxing champ, stepping under the ropes into the ring, with a sea of black faces gazing behind him; smiling confidently, swathed in a silk dressing-gown, a symbol of black power and achievement. . . .

The beauty queen in the bus queue, poised with her umbrella and vanity bag, dazzling and sharply in focus, with the blurred faces of ordinary Africans carrying paper bags in the background, looking round at this apparition of African glory. . . .

The breakfast-table picture, almost compulsory in every number, of an African hero sitting down to a meal with his wife and children in a small location house, like anyone else. . . .

The jazzman, blowing his trumpet or sax in a crazy pose, lying on the floor and kicking his legs in a frenzy, catching the hectic jazz in his movements. . . .

The African businessman sitting at the wheel of his large American car, tremendously sedate and respectable, with a dark suit and a gold tiepin, a picture of success and stability. . . .

Where photographs were a language, juxtaposition was all-important; we could never rely on captions telling a story. The same faces, but different surroundings: the simple girl with the cloth round her hair, opposite the radiant bride; the bus driver opposite the band leader; the nanny opposite the film star: the fashionable socialite opposite the gangster. The contrasts caught the sharp duality of African life, which touched everyone. I could see raw readers looking from the bus driver to the band leader, seeing the same face, and nodding in comprehension.

We could never underestimate the comprehension of our readers. The letters that used to reach the *Drum* office alarmed us all, white and black alike, by their inanity. They were written on advertisements, toilet paper, backs of photographs or envelopes. "Sir, I want to be *Drum*." "Please can I join your *Drum* catalogue?" "*Drum*, please give me *Drum*." "Please, baas, I am *Drum*." Like a child's conversation, playing about with a new-found word. ("I'm a drum, aren't I, Mummy? You're drum too!") We printed a standard reply, absurdly inadequate: "Dear *Drum* reader, thank you for your kind enquiry about *Drum*: we enclose a subscription form, and we hope you will continue to enjoy reading *Drum*."

"*Drum*, please send me six pounds immediately. . . ." "Can I send you a picture of a potato I dug out of my garden? It looks like a little doggie. . . ." "Why don't you give the addresses of girls in *Drum*? The Bible says the truth shall make you free. . . ." "*Drum* makes me very educated, how I lurned much in reading with your *Drum*. . . ."

We started a Knitting Corner on our women's page, and found ourselves bombarded by a persistent correspondence from West Africa, neatly typed and addressed to "Messrs. Knitting Corners", asking us to supply them with large quantities of Knitting Corners for their shop—always very correctly signed. "We are, Sirs, Yours Faithfully, for Soguba Trading Stores, Ltd."

Our readers welcomed any opportunity for misunderstanding. We started a feature contest, with a form asking readers to tick the features they liked best.

Many readers returned the form with YES or DRUM written right across it. We had a popular monthly crossword competition, but several competitors preferred to send the crossword entries to a manufacturer of stoves whose advertisement was opposite. In return we were pestered with demands for anything advertised in *Drum*, or strong hints. "Dear *Drum*, I think Life-buoy is very Good Soap. . . ."

Many of our readers never saw the difference between advertisements and news pages. They thought that any picture of a pretty girl that we published was an advertisement for her services; and, contrarily, that we accepted all advertisements free of charge. One hopeful young man from the Northern Transvaal sent a small grimy snapshot of himself in a bow tie and said: "Please advertise my snap on the *Drum* cover." Later he wrote angrily to ask why we hadn't carried out his instructions.

I ceased to be surprised by anything our readers thought or wrote; I began to wonder at times whether we were not being much sillier than they, trying to foist these bundles of paper on to an unwilling market. Once I watched an old woman discovering with surprise that this funny *Drum* thing actually opened up. That, to her, was the only interesting thing about it.

Very occasionally, we published something in *Drum* which excited our simple readers. We faked a photograph of a man walking down the street with his head under his arm. They loved it. "What happens to his neck when he's taken his head off?" asked one.

Once, in desperation, we tried a campaign of practical jokes. We published a story called "Little Men from the Moon", with photographs of men six inches high, clambering around telephones and climbing up trouser legs. Our readers seemed quite unsurprised: the first two people who rang us up to ask where the moon-men could be found were Europeans. "I wish the moon-men would send their boxers over here to compete with ours," wrote Jerry Pitso from Basutoland.

Perhaps after all the things our readers had seen in Johannesburg—houses on top of each other, white men in moving boxes, and all the white man's magic—they were past being surprised. But I doubt if the white man's magic had ever really surprised them; the story of the blanket-boy gazing in astonishment at the Golden City is, I suspect, a white man's folk-tale, a kind of projected admiration for himself. I remember a doctor telling me how disappointed he was by primitive Zulus seeing an X-ray. They looked at it, understood it, nodded and walked away. I have watched a blanketed Basuto dodging Johannesburg traffic with the bored expression of an American on safari who has seen too much big game, when his car is held up by lions.

The most exciting event to these people during my time as editor was not the Defiance Campaign in which eight thousand Africans went to jail, nor the tornado which swept up half an African location and lifted cars in the air, nor the Port Elizabeth riots when four white men were murdered and a cinema gutted—but the discovery of Tokoloshe—a kind of Zulu imp—in a location of Johannesburg. Before it had been mentioned in the papers, the news reached every location on the Reef in twelve hours. Wild rumours spread. It had been found brewing beer in a backyard. It belonged to a witch doctor. It was disguised as a monkey. When the papers came out with news of the Tokoloshe, they sold three times their usual number. Eventually the Tokoloshe was found. It was an otter.

We started a feature called Heartbreaks, on the pattern of European magazines, and invited readers to send in their problems to "Dolly Drum". Heartbreaks became one of the most popular pages in the magazine, but the problems were baffling in their confusion and silliness. Dolly, who was a worried syndicate of men, became almost as confused as her readers. We tried all kinds of people for the job—a missionary, but he was too severe; Henry, but he was too frivolous; myself, but I was too patronising. Being Dolly was a job that everyone tried to escape. We ended by discussing the trickier problems round the office.

"Here's someone in Orlando who wants a second wife."

"Tell him he can't love two women at once."

"Why not? I can."

Polygamy was one of Dolly's recurring problems. Under tribal custom, a man could have as many wives as he could afford; he paid *lobola* or bride-price to each father-in-law. The system still survives, and even Arthur had to pay *lobola* for his wife. But most of our readers were married by Christian rites, and their education was Christian. The conflict between the two traditions was obvious in the letters:

I am a young man in Kenya in a responsible position and earning a good salary. I am married and have two children. But my wife doesn't obey me, and I want to divorce her. Not long ago I was going to the country on business and asked her to make me some provision, but she refused. So I think I need a second wife who will live in a different bungalow but obey my instructions. How should I do it, Dolly, please?

I'm thirty and married for fourteen years, but my wife has never had a baby. I came to work in Johannesburg two years ago and met another woman with whom I have a lovely little child. I love my wife and I love the mother of my child. How can I bring them together and live happily with them?

Then there was the old problem of *lobola*: was a girl really worth that much?

Here I am, in love with a girl three years my junior. We want to get married, but her parents are asking for a very high sum for dowry, which will take me nine months to earn. Should I take all that trouble or should I leave her? [asked "Puzzled" of Brakpan]

Race was a recurring theme:

I am an African girl living in a small town in Natal [said "Helpless"]. I have had a lot of African boyfriends, and I had a raw deal from all of them. Their manners are bad, and they treat me badly. They have sometimes gone out of their way to be rude to me, and think nothing of scolding me in the presence of other people. A year ago I met a Coloured man. He is such a gentleman. I am completely mad about him. Whenever I go out with him, African men make rude remarks, and this makes me feel ashamed that I am an African. They have threatened to beat me up should they see me with him again. But, Dolly, what can I do? I hate the men of my race, as long as I live I will never have anything to do with them. Why don't they leave me alone?

A more tragic cry came from Northern Rhodesia:

> My sister and I are Bemba girls, and we both have bwana
> husbands [white lovers]. We love each other very much. But
> my husband Piet says that if his father catches him with me,
> he will shoot him. Piet says he will do anything to be with
> me. Please, Dolly, what can we do? Where can we be safe?
> Can we go to Congo or England? Please, Dolly, tell me what
> we can do.

Dolly could not publish this letter, and she could not face the
reply.

Indians, Coloureds and Europeans had more money than
African men, which sometimes increased, temporarily, their
attraction:

> I am twenty-two and in love with an Indian boy. He is
> twenty-five and a shopkeeper and always gives me articles
> from his shop free of charge; but my parents don't know
> about this. I have just found out that I don't love him deeply
> enough. Do you think if I reject him he will want his articles
> back? [asked "Bewildered" of Beroni]

Dolly's correspondents were all bewildered. They were uprooted from their strict tribal discipline, and not yet adjusted to
Western customs. The poverty of the reserves, the compound
system, the instability of Africans in towns, and the wretched
lack of housing, had all contributed to a promiscuous, rootless
existence. "Propose" meant propose for the night, and
"husband" meant lover or sleeping-partner. "I will love you
for ever," meant until tomorrow morning. Some teachers with
their girl pupils revealed new depths of immorality; but Dolly
could never be shocked:

We are two schoolgirls, aged seventeen and eighteen respectively. We have just discovered that we are going to be mothers, and the man responsible is a teacher at a neighbouring school. We are still scholars and do not know what to do because this man cannot marry both of us. How can we solve this?

"Please, Dolly! Help, Dolly! My last hope, Dolly! Dolly, what can I do, where can I go?" I could almost hear these cries of bewilderment from the shanty towns of the Reef. What could Dolly do? Their lives were so unstable and disrupted that no reply from Dolly could make sense. "It's time you settled down, my dear. . . ." Dolly would say, from her lofty plane, in reply to "Miss Worried" of Orlando Shelters; but I could imagine Miss Worried reading it in her one-room windowless hovel, with her married boy-friend saying: "Baby, I'll make you pregnant first, then I'll marry you, true's God!"

Occasionally, Dolly scored a victory.

My boy-friend has made me pregnant, but I don't want to have a baby [said "Distressed"]. He says I should have an abortion. Tell me, Dolly, is it dangerous?

Dolly was firm, and would not think of an abortion. Six months later came a letter:

In the January *Drum*, the problem I sent you appeared in your Heartbreaks column under the heading "Is it Dangerous?" I now have a chubby baby boy, whom I love very much. I shudder to think what I was thinking to do when you gave me the advice which changed my whole outlook towards my problem. Everything is under control now. I am going back to nursing in September. Thanks a million Dolly Drum. May the other readers whom you will advise gain by it as I have.

Sometimes readers gave *us* advice:

> Here are a few words I would like to tell all my friends
> through your widely-read magazine [wrote Solomon Idowu
> of Lagos]. Can a woman love you for your poor life? No,
> without a penny, woman cannot love you, sir! Women are
> many, and here is their doing. When poverty comes in at the
> door, love flies out at the window.

CHAPTER NINE

Come Back Africa

Drum originally announced that it would be non-political, and the first issues made no mention of politics. With Malan's government in power, and tension high, there was much to be said for avoiding so dangerous a subject. In addition, *Drum*'s staff, proprietor included, were not politically minded.

"If I went in for politics, I would be the most dangerous man in Africa," said Can. "I would be cunning and ruthless and I would stop at nothing. The boys are always imploring me to go into politics. 'We need you, Can,' they say. . . ."

"And why don't you?"

"Fifty-five pounds a month; that's why. I'm what they call a sell-out."

But however much we tried to ignore them, in South Africa all roads led to politics. Political theory affected every moment of our readers' lives: it could have them arrested, jailed, transplanted, even deported.

As *Drum* came closer to its readers, the lack of politics appeared more serious. "How can you claim to represent the African people," asked a reader, "if you don't represent their politics?"

We decided to survey the field cautiously. I soon became engrossed in the little-known subject of African politics. By far the most important African political organisation was the African National Congress.

Congress was founded in 1912 by a determined Zulu lawyer, Dr. Pixley Seme, to protect African rights in the newly-formed Union of South Africa. In its first years, led by staid and respectable African ministers, lawyers and scholars, Congress pursued a moderate course of protests and petitions. After two unsuccessful delegations to England in 1914 and 1919, they realised that Britain was not prepared to intercede on their behalf; but they continued to appeal to the South African governments against infringements of their rights.

After Cape Africans were deprived of their vote in 1936, Congress began to lose faith in white governments; and during the war, with new talk of racial equality and freedom of opportunity, the voice of African Nationalism became louder. The Congress Youth League, inspired by an able young law graduate, Anton Lembede, pressed Congress leadership towards greater militancy. The election of Malan to power in 1948 put an end to any hopes that Congress might have of concessions from whites. Thereafter, militancy won steadily over moderation.

The election of Dr. Moroka to succeed Dr. Xuma as President in 1949 marked a new phase in Congress. Moroka, though himself a conservative by nature, was the candidate of the militant Youth League, and a figurehead for their bolder policies. Congress was committed to uncompromising opposition to the government.

Up till 1950, Congress was frankly Nationalist, and frequently anti-white and anti-Indian in its attitude. They were opposed to Communists, with their inter-racial theories and allegiance to Moscow; and Communists accused Congress of being bourgeois and racialist. But after the Suppression of Communism Act of 1950, many African Communists took refuge in Congress. African Nationalists and Communists combined, albeit uneasily, in common cause against the government; Congress dropped, ostensibly at least, its exclusive Nationalism, and allied itself with the South African Indian Congress and, later, with the European Congress of Democrats. The Youth League, though black Nationalism remained its driving force, began to show some

103

of the trappings of Communism. Since all African politicians began to be considered by whites as Communists, the fundamental differences between Communists and Nationalists became blurred.

*   *   *

In December, 1951, I travelled down to Bloemfontein with Jurgen and Henry, to attend the thirty-fifth annual meeting of Congress. At the time we did not realise that this meeting would be of deep significance for the future of South Africa.

It was held in a bare hall in the African location of Bloemfontein, and was due to begin at nine. At ten, people began wandering up and chatting outside. A few drove up in cars, and a lorry load of Africans arrived.

Two hours late, three hundred people trooped lazily into the hall, a Press table was hurriedly improvised for us and two other white journalists from the local paper. Henry pointed to the important people, and Jurgen photographed them. Most of them had never been photographed before, and some objected. Everything seemed obscure and dingy.

On the platform was the suave President-General of Congress, Dr. James Sebebubijwasegokgobontharile Moroka, light-skinned and well dressed. "He's a very wealthy man," said Henry. "He's just driven up from his Free State farm in his Plymouth." His middle name meant "one who is entangled in a cobweb". Dr. Molema, the Treasurer of Congress, explained that it signified "criminally enslaved and oppressed". Moroka's enemies said it meant "politically confused".

Near Moroka was a small ascetic-looking man, with a calm wizened face. "That's Manilal Gandhi," said Henry, "the son of the Mahatma; he's come up from Natal."

The meeting began. Everyone sang the Congress anthem, "Noosi Sikelel'i Afrika." The whole hall vibrated with the rhythm of the melancholy song:

God bless Africa
Raise up our descendants
Hear our prayers.
Lord, bless us.
Come, holy spirit,
Come, holy spirit,
Lord bless us,
Us your children.

I watched the faces of the crowd, transformed by passion. A delicate little clergyman with a tiny goatee beard, straining his thin throat with singing; a ragged old man swinging his arms to the rhythm, gazing rapturously at the rafters; a bulging woman shouting the song with indignation in every syllable. I noticed, to my surprise, a meek-looking messenger who delivered packages to *Drum* singing earnestly among the crowd. He came up to me afterwards. "Please, baas, don't tell my baas that you saw me here. . . ."

As the last harmonies of the song died down, Moroka lifted up his thumb and shouted: *Mayibuye!* The crowd shouted: *Afrika!*—pronouncing the word in the African way, with long a's. "Mayibuye Afrika—that means 'Come back Africa'," explained Henry. "It's one of the slogans of Congress; it means back to the old days of freedom before the white man came."

The meeting went on for three days. The hall became hotter, and the speeches longer. I wondered why I had come.

And then a report was read, from a joint-planning council of the African National Congress and the South African Indian Congress.[1] It recommended that the government should be asked to repeal "six unjust laws" early in 1952. If they were not repealed, Congress should embark on a defiance campaign of passive resistance against those laws, not later than June 26, 1952.

[1] The S.A.I.C., founded by Mahatma Gandhi in 1908, is the principal political body of the 365,000 Indians in South Africa.

The report was passed.

Would Congress carry out their spectacular threat? People seemed doubtful.

"Before an army goes to war, it must learn to march in step," said Dr. Alfred Xuma, himself an ex-President of Congress.

"Cooperating with Indians is like a dying man hanging on to a shark," said Richard Selope-Thema, leader of the "national-minded bloc" in Congress.

"Congress leaders haven't got the true spirit of sacrifice," said Manilal Gandhi.

After the meeting, we passed through Maseru, in Basutoland, and I called on a young judicial commissioner in the colonial service, Patrick Duncan. He was a Wykehamist, and a son of Sir Patrick Duncan, a former Governor-General of South Africa.

I found him discussing Gandhi with a bishop. He had been reading the Mahatma's autobiography, *Experiments in Truth*. Pat asked me eagerly about the Congress meeting:

"So they're really planning a passive resistance campaign? Gosh, I wish I'd been there. . . . What did Manilal think?" Pat gave me a copy of *Satyagraha in South Africa*, the book by the Mahatma describing his passive resistance campaign, in Johannesburg in 1908, against Smuts.

"If only Congress can adopt Gandhi's methods. . . ." said Pat, as we left. He seemed to be one of the few Europeans who took the defiance resolution seriously.

Six months later, on June 26, 1952, the defiance campaign broke on an unsuspecting South Africa. Congress jumped suddenly into the world headlines.

A small group of Indians and Africans, led by a veteran Gandhi-ist, Nana Sita, wearing a white "Gandhi cap", walked in a long line into the African location of Boksburg, near Johannesburg, without entry permits.

They wore the Congress colours on their arms: black for the

people, green for the land, yellow for the gold—and held their thumbs up in the Congress salute, singing "Jan Van Riebeck[1] has stolen our freedom." They walked into the police, who arrested them, bundled them into a troop carrier and took them to cells.

The same evening Congress held a meeting at the Garment Workers' Hall in Johannesburg. At eleven o'clock, the beginning of the curfew, a procession of Africans marched out of the hall into Anderson Street; across both ends of the street stood a row of police, shoulder to shoulder, peering beneath their helmets at this meek band of Africans deliberately defying the curfew.

A police officer spoke to Yusuf Cachalia, the Secretary of the Indian Congress, who was marshalling the Africans. Cachalia's languid composure contrasted with the officer's tense look. The groups of "defiers", standing in their rows like football teams, climbed happily into the waiting police lorries singing *Nkosi Sikelele*, and were driven away, while the police looked on.

The first day set the pattern for the campaign. In the next five months, eight thousand people went to jail, for one to three weeks; they marched into locations, walked out after curfew, travelled in European railway coaches, entered stations by European entrances. Everywhere they marched quietly and did what they were told by the police, singing hymns with their thumbs up. They always informed the police beforehand, to make sure they would be arrested.

White South Africa was alarmed. These batches of volunteers springing up all over the country, marching peacefully to jail, upset the traditional European view of Africans as being either savage or incapable of organisation. "The significance of the Defiance Campaign," said the Johannesburg *Star*, "was in fact that there were more than 7,500 non-Europeans prepared to go to jail—that no incident had been provoked. This implied a

[1] Van Riebeck, who landed in the Cape in 1652, was the founder of white South Africa.

confidence and a discipline which nobody expected of the native people."[1]

The campaign caught the imagination of Africans. "Mayibuye—Afrika," with thumbs up, became a greeting in the street. Politics began to rival boxing in popularity with our readers. In October, 1952, *Drum* published an eight-page photographic history of the campaign. The number sold out at sixty-five thousand and reached a new circulation peak. Copies were resold at double the price.

Malan's government was determined to stamp out the campaign. Congress offices and homes were raided, documents seized. Dr. Moroka was arrested at his surgery at Thaba 'Nchu, and charged under the Suppression of Communism Act. "I do not know the specific nature of the crimes I am alleged to have committed," said Moroka, "but my lawyer is trying to find out." With him were arrested nineteen other Indian and African Congress leaders. They were tried and convicted, under the wide powers of the act, of "statutory Communism", and given a suspended sentence. "This has nothing to do with Communism as it is commonly known," said Mr. Justice Rumpff in sentencing them.

Then, in mid-November, 1952, Pat Duncan wrote to me, saying that he had decided to join the defiance campaign.

I visited him the following weekend; he had left the colonial service, moved over the border from Basutoland into South Africa, and bought a farm and a mail-order bookshop.

He was recovering from a leg injury, and limped round the garden on crutches, talking with enthusiasm.

"I *can't* let this campaign fade out without showing that there are whites that support it," he said. "I'm *convinced* that passive resistance is the solution, but it mustn't become anti-white. . . ."

Pat came up to Johannesburg, where Congress had arranged for him to "defy" with six other Europeans, and a mixed group

[1] Johannesburg *Star*. 6/1/53.

of Africans and Indians. Just before his "defiance" was due, Pat had lunch with his friend Manilal Gandhi. Manilal had always disapproved of Congress, and said that the campaign was not in the true spirit of sacrifice. "Then it's our job to change it," argued Pat. At the end of lunch Manilal agreed to join Pat in his defiance.

On the hot afternoon of December 2, an odd little party of seven whites, and thirty-two Indians and Africans, gathered at the entrance to Germiston location, near Johannesburg. None of them had permits to enter the location. At the appointed time, Pat walked slowly into the dusty location on his crutches, looking strained and anxious, with the Congress colours fluttering from one crutch. Next to him, with calm, half-shut eyes, walked Manilal Gandhi; beside and behind them were spruce clean-shaven young Africans and Indians, and European women. Round the little procession ran the journalists and photographers. The black children in the rough location streets looked up in astonishment at this slow march through their playground. Behind them drove the police, in cars.

In the middle of the location Pat stopped, turned round to the crowd of Africans who were following the procession, and spoke to them in Sesuto (which he had learnt as a child from the servants at Government House):

"Today South African people of all kinds have come among you. They have come with love for you and with peace. I ask you to do what you have to do without making trouble, but in a spirit of love. Mayibuye! Afrika! . . ."

The crowd shouted "Afrika!" in reply, and the women warbled their high-pitched cry of welcome.

The procession moved on, back to the location entrance, where police were waiting. They were questioned, arrested and driven off to the police station. Pat's wife Cynthia handed Pat a toothbrush and an Afrikaans Bible as he stepped into the police car.

When the seven white prisoners, with Manilal Gandhi, came

up before the court, they were charged, not with breaking the permit regulations which they intended to defy, but with inciting natives to break the law, in terms of a new promulgation which had just been rushed through. Pat was found guilty, and sentenced to six weeks. On a question of principle, they appealed, but as the appeal dragged on, they withdrew, and Pat eventually served two weeks of his sentence. "We bungled it," said Pat afterwards. "We should never have appealed."

The procession in Germiston, led by the Governor General's son and the Mahatma's son, brought new significance to the campaign. "Pat's offer to defy," said Yusuf Cachalia, "came as a gift from Heaven: it stopped the campaign becoming racial."

To the world overseas, Pat's defiance gave the campaign a new prestige and respectability: to white South Africa, Pat gave it a new horror. The name of Duncan was revered by South Africans. "It makes you think, when an educated chap like that joins with the natives," said one of our compositors.

As never before, I felt the chasm between white South Africa and England. It was strange to turn from editorials in South African papers, condemning the campaign as a grave threat to law and order, to a copy of the London *Times*, containing an appeal signed by distinguished names, for funds to help the campaign.

In December, 1952, Congress held its thirty-sixth annual meeting. Pat was the guest of honour. Moroka, whose term of office had expired, came up for re-election; but his popularity had waned, and he had shown misgivings about the campaign. Albert John Luthuli was elected President of Congress, by one hundred and fifty votes to forty-seven.

Luthuli was in great contrast to Moroka: he was a large dark Zulu, with a flat face and rugged features. He spoke English haltingly, feeling for words, gesturing with his large hands. He outlined his policy simply: "Never to resort to force, to invite more Europeans to volunteer, and to allow nothing to stand in the way of my people's freedom. . . ."

"We always used to regard Luthuli as a 'mission boy'," said an elder statesman of Congress. Luthuli grew up at the Groutville mission station in Natal, where his father was an interpreter; later he taught at Adams College, run by the American board mission; he visited India in 1938 as a delegate to the International Missionary Society; and in 1948 he lectured in America about missions in Africa, as a guest of the American board mission.

But Luthuli felt that his main duty to his people lay in politics. In 1951 he was elected President of the Natal branch of Congress, and he took a major part in the planning of the defiance campaign. The government summoned him to Pretoria, and asked him to choose between leaving Congress or resigning from his chieftainship. He resigned.

Soon after his election as President of Congress, Luthuli made a statement which summed up his predicament.

"Who will deny that thirty years of my life have been spent knocking in vain, patiently, moderately and modestly, at a closed and barred door?

"What have been the fruits of my many years of moderation? The past thirty years have seen the greatest number of laws restricting our rights and progress, until today we have reached a stage where we have almost no rights at all.

"It is with this background . . . that I have joined my people in the new spirit which moves them today, the spirit that revolts openly and boldly against injustice and expresses itself in a determined and non-violent manner.

"This stand of mine, which resulted in my being sacked from the chieftainship, might seem foolish and disappointing to some liberal and moderate Europeans and non-Europeans with whom I have worked these many years, and with whom I still hope to work. This is no parting of the ways but a launching farther into the deep. I invite them to join us in our unequivocal pronouncement of all legitimate African aspirations and in our firm stand against injustice and oppression. The wisdom or foolishness of this decision I place in the hands of the Almighty."[1]

* * *

The government was determined to stamp out Congress activity. Using the wide powers of the suppression of communism act, it barred Congress leaders from meetings, confined them to their own districts, forbade them to hold office and even, in two cases, deported them.

In January, 1953, the Minister of Justice introduced two new acts which were designed finally to crush the defiance campaign. The first of them, the public safety act, would enable the Governor General to declare a state of emergency whenever "the maintenance of public order was endangered", during which time he could issue regulations which would suspend existing laws. The second act, the criminal law amendment act, laid down severe penalties for anyone inciting others to commit offences by way of protest, or soliciting financial assistance for organised protest. The maximum penalties were a fine of £500, or five years' imprisonment, or ten lashes, or any combination of two of these.

When the new Bills came before Parliament, the official opposition, the United Party, decided after a long session in caucus to support them. Only eight M.P.s voted against them.

"Tomorrow," said the veteran Senator Heaton Nicholls, "we will virtually be in a police state. . . ."

* * *

In face of the new penalties, the defiance campaign ended almost as suddenly as it had begun. The six months' wonder passed quickly into history. Most of its leaders were convicted of being "statutory communists" and banned from office.

How far, in fact, was Congress communist-inspired? I put the

[1] The Friend. 16/1/53.

question to Luthuli at his home in Natal, to which he was confined by the government.

"What South Africa is hearing from Congress," said Luthuli, "is the voice of African nationalism, not communism. African nationalism will become a much more powerful and appealing force than communism. In fact, our task as leaders is to make this nationalism a broad one, rather than the narrow nationalism of the Afrikaner Nationalist party. Extreme nationalism is a greater danger than communism, and a more real one. . . .

"So long as Congress members subscribe to our policy, we do not care about their political affiliations. We welcome anyone who is working with us for freedom. It is true that there are many ex-communists in Congress today; but that does not mean for a moment that Congress is communist; if I were convinced that Congress was working for Moscow, I would definitely resign. . . .

"At the moment we are only concerned with rescuing ourselves out of the mire; and we cannot yet say which direction we shall follow after that. For myself, I would wish for socialism, in the British sense—if I were in England I would vote Labour. But in Congress we have people of many different political beliefs—capitalists, socialists, and the rest. . . . No, Communism is not a serious menace to South Africa."

If Communism was not a serious menace, the government was determined to try to make it one. By calling all their enemies Communists, they not only paid the Communist Party an undeserved compliment, but concealed genuine Communism among a heap of staid and conservative "statutory Communists".

"Are you a Communist?" an African asked me at a party.

"No. Why should I be?"

"Oh, by Communist, I mean a friend of the Africans."

CHAPTER TEN

House of Truth

"Ladies and gentlemen! Let me present to you Africa's greatest film star, the irresistible, incomparable, indescribable one and only—Dolly Rathebe!"

I was sitting on a hard chair in a barely-furnished room in Sophiatown, lit by an uncertain paraffin lamp in one corner. The dirty green walls were flaking away, showing the plaster underneath; the only decoration was a crude four-colour calendar of a reclining blonde, advertising a Johannesburg garage, and a murky photograph of a stern and pious African grandmother, in a heavy oval frame. In one corner was a wobbly wardrobe, with a pile of clothes and boxes on top of it; in another corner a few crates were stacked on each other.

Round the room, thirty people were sitting in silence. They had been sitting for an hour in this deep, brooding African silence, gazing in front of them without expression or expectation. At the back were the old people—older than Johannesburg, their eyes looking tired with so many years of gazing. No one had tried to break the silence.

I was in a corner, the only white man, with friends on either side. I had forgotten that I was white. Only once, when I noticed my white hand next to a black hand, like a black note on a piano, did the oddness strike me.

I knew many of the people in the room—Todd in the other corner, Henry wandering outside, Can, our host, flitting lightly round the room. I wondered if anything would happen in this impassive gathering. But no one seemed worried by the silence.

Suddenly Can, the master of ceremonies, climbed on a chair; his slender body was quivering with energy, as if compelled by some electric shock. He gathered his academic gown around him, his own Bachelor of Arts gown from Fort Hare; and announced with confident authority the one and only Dolly Rathebe.

The spectators stared up at him with looks of scepticism. And they were right, for Dolly was not there. The silence was broken. "She got bored!" "She went that-a-way!" "Go fetch her, man!" "Voetsak!" Can remained calm. "Ladies and gentlemen, Miss Rathebe will be with us very shortly. . . ."

Sure enough, just then, Dolly appeared at the doorway. She had an instant effect on the crowd. For Dolly was the most famous African girl in the whole continent: her face appeared on hoardings, in films, and in *Drum*: she sang in white night clubs and made records which sold all over Africa. Yet here she was, the great Dolly, our Dolly, in the doorway of a small room in Sophiatown.

She was looking very beautiful, in her exotic way. She wore a long black dress, low cut, her brown shoulders and head emerging like a sculpted bust, hewn and rounded and polished from soft brown stone. Her thick black hair, gathered round with beads, stood up severely from her forehead; and she held herself erect on her high-heeled shoes, like a statue, with the disdain of a *grande dame*, poised with an unshakeable dignity in these undignified surroundings.

She stood there, with her big knowing eyes roving round the room. Then she smiled a naughty smile, and let out a tiny high-pitched giggle, and put her hand to her mouth in mimicked shame. She looked quickly again round the room: no longer the statue on her pedestal, but the warm peasant girl, unspoilt, unprotected, among her people. "Dolly, girl!" "There's my baby!" "Katz!" "Doll-Doll!" shouted the crowd; and she giggled again with delight, her small rounded face warm in the flickering light, her wide white teeth shining from the dark in open friendliness. The spectators jumped up and down on their chairs in anticipation.

She spoke quietly, three octaves lower than her giggle, seeming to come right from the middle of her long brown body.

"Did you boys want to see me?" she giggled again, three octaves up. Everyone shouted: "Ya!" "Sure things!" "True's God!" "Hi, Dolly, girl!"

Dolly walked across the room, sophisticated as a mannequin, and yet with the simple poise and grace of a Xhosa girl walking across open country with a pitcher full of water balanced on her head. She whispered to Todd, who looked businesslike and serious as only Todd could. He hummed a long note. Dolly squeaked again. Todd hummed again. Dolly sang a pure low note, and Todd nodded with gravity.

Dolly stepped out, her fine shoulders pulled back, her tinsel ear-rings flashing in the light against her dark, flat ears. She stood still. Abruptly, her face lit up, her eyes twinkled, and every limb sprang into movement. She leant forward on her toes, heaved her breasts forward, lifted up her arms, with her fingers tense, ready to strangle. Her mouth opened wide, her big lips quivered, and she burst into song.

She sang the Xhosa hit-tune, "Into Yam", which had sent the Reef locations crazy with delight. The song was about a girl who loved her man although he was a drunkard; the words jumped out with a frenzied desperation, beating the stark rhythm which repeated itself again and again like a broken record.

> I love my thing!
> Cos my man's my thing!
> Call him drink drank drunk!
> He's still my thing!
> He jobs for me!
> That you wouldn't have thunk!
> So I love my thing!
> Ee Ma Yee Mo Wunk!

Instantly the stone-faced figures round the room sprang to life like puppets lifted off their perch. Their eyes lit up and their feet beat time, and they clapped as one man, with the beat of the music; they wailed the accompaniment which zig-zagged through the tune, or blew imaginary trombones, or twanged non-existent guitars.

Can, still twirling his gown around him, stepped into the middle of the floor, hopping to the rhythm like a clockwork duck: his whole body twisted into a sharp curve; one hand curled up behind his back, the other, tense with expression, gripped into his side. His feet jerked as if on hot coals; his body was consumed with the rhythm, lost to the world around him like an epileptic. His tongue slid between his teeth, and his face was contorted in a grimace.

Twenty other bodies were now up and jiving on the floor, hopping to and from each other, grinning and gasping in a crazy silent conversation.

I sat in my corner, watching this mass of dancing bodies. Everything was changed. The green peeling walls seemed insubstantial, swaying in time with the music. Grandma in the oval frame took on a new expression of tolerance and sympathy. The room became vast, its sharp right-angles vague and distant. The jivers seemed not solid.

Europe was translated into Africa. Every movement, every look, had the touch and feel of Africa. As I walked across the room in my European way, I felt like a corpse striding out from the grave.

One old man sat in the empty chair next to me; I turned to him. "Are you enjoying this?" He jumped up with the shock.

"It is not right, sir, do you understand, for the African people to behave like this before a European? What will the Europeans think of us?" He pronounced the "Ahfrican people" as if he were a visiting anthropologist.

The music throbbed on, issuing mysteriously from the

wobbling bodies, steady as a record. I focused on the figures tugging and flinging each other just near me. Behind the frenzied movements I could detect drama. Johnny, a smooth, light-skinned African, was jiving ecstatically with a young dark girl whose eyes followed his everywhere, and whose small feet jerked to and fro in neat obedience to his. But Johnny's quick eye kept jiving to a long-haired Coloured girl, embroiled in a solemn dance with a spectacled teacher; and her eyes were always waiting for his. Their eyes quickly met, and flicked away, and Johnny gave a look of knowing.

A couple, hugged in a tight dance, lost to the world, suddenly, with no word said, walked away in opposite directions to sit down. A school principal with enormous spectacles, looking disapproving at the side, suddenly hopped up and shook his nimble legs in all directions.

The singing stopped: not the end of a record, but the current switched off. The jiving stopped. The clapping stopped. Everybody separated and sat down.

Can, frozen in an apoplexy of jive, walked sedately towards me, with a large bearded man looking like a tamed cannibal chief.

"Tony, I'd like to introduce you," said Can with mock pomposity, waving his arm at the man with the beard, "to a friend of mine—we call him the Bearded Horror—Horror for short. He's just left Fort Hare, and he's working in a bookshop. He's very interested in Bach, and he wants to write an article for *Drum*."

Horror smiled shyly, the pink inside of his lips looking pale against the brown skin and black beard. He sat down, and we talked about Fort Hare and customers at bookshops.

As we talked, as in the interval of a play, I watched people coming in and out. Johnny, his large sensuous mouth dropping with boredom, turned over records on top of the gramophone. Then he turned round, caught the eye of the Coloured girl, and ambled slowly out of the room, his hands deep in his pockets; two minutes later, the Coloured girl rose and went out, looking purposeful and domestic. I did not see them again.

Henry appeared from the next room, benign and paternal, surveying the room as if surprised that the party had continued without him. He came up to me laughing at the continuous joke of our relationship, and said: "Are you all right?" He went up to Todd, slipping off his chair in the excitement of a jazz argument.

"Todd, can I have a word with you outside?" Henry whispered importantly.

"No, man! Can't you see I'm busy, man?" said Todd briskly, and turned quickly back. "Shucks, Paddy, boy, but you can't compare the Swingsters to the Maniacs! The Maniacs are dead!"

Henry walked on magnanimously.

Can reappeared in the room, his arm round a meek bird-faced man carrying a case. A shout of "Jazzboy!" echoed all round, in every pitch and intonation. "Jazzboy Jazzboy, Jazzboy, Jazzboy!" The little man smiled a conjuror's smile, opened his case, and produced a gleaming saxophone while jazz fiends pranced round him, fondling his instrument, and shouting his name like a spell. "Blow it, Jazzboy! Show 'em, Jazzboy! Let it go, Jazzboy!" He stood upright with his proud instrument hanging from a black cord round his neck, as confident now as a soldier in uniform, and blew a swift arpeggio, lingering on a high shrill note which could crack the room in two.

Can, glowing with achievement, climbed again on to the chair.

"Ladies and gentlemen! I have the honour to present to you the renowned famous notorious well-known star of the Metronomes, Jazzboy!" And the word echoed again round the room.

"But before Jazzboy starts blowing," Can shouted above the noise, "I come to the solemn business of this evening." Can gathered his robes. "We have come here this evening to perform

119

a solemn onerous duty. We have come to christen this noble mansion." He waved round at the peeling walls and the shaky furniture. "Gentlemen, I have the honour tonight to name this palace 'The House of Truth'!"

The spectators shouted: "Truth! The House of Truth!" Can cut a streamer and the two ends fluttered down; there was cheering and clapping and more cries of "Truth! The House of Truth!"

I turned to P-boy, a young student sitting near me. "Why is it called the House of Truth?"

"It's a long story! You see, every room in Sophiatown has to have a name. I live in the House of Commons; Johnny lives in the House of Saints. But this place is very special, Mr. Sampson. You see, everyone in this room is supposed to speak the truth. No bull, no yes-men! Particularly with regard to—Love!"

"Over to Jazzboy!" shouted Can.

Jazzboy's sax shrieked jazz, and the bodies round the room were galvanised into jive. Horror turned to me.

"Do you know what this tune is called? It's called 'Bambata'. Do you know who Bambata was?"

"No."

"He was a Zulu king who led a rebellion against the white men. We always call our songs after African heroes," he added dryly.

"Bambata" pounded on. Jazzboy, impassive and intent, blew tirelessly. David stood by him, possessive of his hero, staring at the shining brass. The dramas of the jivers picked up again.

Henry performed a vertical solo jive in the corner, as if pulling down an imaginary rope and treading soil at the same time. I noticed my grave old man, so concerned with the dignity of the Ahfrican people, jiving with his knees bent double, half-seas over in the middle of the floor.

Jazzboy, his face a balloon and his eyes rolling into white, paraded slowly round the room. David and the jivers followed him, as solemnly as if they were following Bambata himself. Jazzboy played in turn to the seated guests, and lingered in front of Horror and me, bowing so that the wind shook Horror's kinky beard, and adding special twiddles to the bare tune in our honour.

"Ladies and gentlemen," shouted Can, above the din. "Before we continue any further—the toast." And there was silence.

"To Oubaas," said Can. There was a pause, and then every-one chanted together, in unison:

> The son of a bitch
> Had no right to lead
> Such a dangerous life.

I remembered Oubaas well. The "old boss" was a young man of twenty-five who seemed old and wise enough to be fifty; he had been very much part of this gang. He had mediated in quarrels, patched up love affairs, organised parties and kept out gangsters. He was an intellectual, steeped in Shakespeare and with pages of poetry in his head; but he led the same rough life of danger of any other Sophiatowner. "I cannot praise a fugitive and cloistered virtue," he would say. I had last seen him reading the *Divine Comedy* in his leaking shack in Sophiatown. A month ago he had been killed in a car crash.

". . . Such a dangerous life. . . ." The solemnity lingered, and then Jazzboy lifted up his sax again and blew a gale into it.

Near me, primly alone, was a pretty little Xhosa girl, mani-cured and powdered to make her face light; she looked innocent and demure. The spectacled teacher came up to her and sat beside her. With elaborate courtesy he opened his shining cigarette case.

"Will you have a de Reszke, Princess?"

"Thank you, but I never ever smoke a cigarette, Mr. Tshabalala."

121

I turned round to Horror.

"She's very young and sweet, isn't she?"

"She's the biggest little bitch in Sophiatown," said Horror feelingly. I saw Princess beckon to Can, who danced obediently up to her.

"Canny, boy, can I have a speak with you?"

"But naturally, my Princess, I'd be de-lighted."

They both walked out of the room. A minute later, Can came back and whispered to P-boy, who was chatting gaily with two girls. P-boy laughed and threw up his hands in mock despair. He made extravagant excuses to the two girls, and then waltzed out of the room, his features sad.

Can sat down next to me, and we talked gravely about next month's *Drum*, shouting above blasts of noise.

"POLICE!"

It was David, shouting from the window behind us. The jazz stopped. In the corner, someone drained his glass and put a bottle of brandy under a floorboard. Can, radiating respectability, walked slowly towards the door.

"This way, Mr. Sampson," said David, pushing up the window. I tried to look dignified. I reminded myself that I was here on business. I knew that I was within the law. But I remembered that the police disliked white men in black townships. I looked at Can, who looked at me. He nodded.

I stumbled to the window. Everyone laughed and pushed me on, and heaved me outside. "There goes Tony!" "You ought to be black!" they shouted gaily.

In the darkness, David grabbed me, and pointed to a dustbin.

"I'd better go back." He disappeared.

I crouched behind the stinking dustbin. It was very uncomfortable. I could see the lighted room through the window; the jazz had started again. I felt the full force of apartheid.

I found a more comfortable position; lit a cigarette, and felt that perhaps this incident was not the final humiliation of the editor, but his triumph. I began to have the feeling of Sophiatown, sharing this moment of anxiety with my readers: here, in this stinking corner, waiting for the crunch of boots and the shout of "Voetsak, man!" watching the jazz House of Truth through the window, I had a moment of truth. How easy to understand those short stories I read and discarded every day, obsessed with race and violence, in single-minded bitterness. How compulsory was this floating cabin of jazz and jive.

David appeared and shouted: "Tony!" (He usually called me, very formally, Mr. Sampson.) "It's okay, they've gone!"

I rose and stretched my legs; we smiled at each other in silent understanding of the situation. He opened the window, and pushed me up, back into the room. Everyone looked round; somebody shouted, "The native!" and the room laughed. Can came up to me, beaming, and dusted my coat.

"They've gone?" I asked.

"Ya! And the joke is, they only came to try and bum a drink."

I looked at my watch, and noticed with a shock that it was half-past midnight. I went up to Can.

"It's been a great evening. Thank you."

"De-lighted. But wait till the tenth. And you whites want to get rid of Sophiatown!"

I slipped out silently, taking a last glance at the crowded room. Jazzboy was now lying on the floor, still blowing his sax, with jivers all around him. The old men were still sitting along the back, gazing in front of them.

I walked outside into the stinking yard, past tiny shacks of corrugated iron leaning against the brick buildings; through the chinks in the iron I could see candlelight, and hear people talking. As I walked through the yard I could hear familiar voices whispering from the darkness—Princess, P-boy, Johnny, the Coloured girl. By the gate out to the road, Horror was leaning on the post, watching the gangs of hooligans passing up and down the street.

CHAPTER ELEVEN

Whites

"Nanku umlungu!" "There's a white man among us!" I heard
as I wandered through the African locations. I began to see
myself as something of a freak: with this pale albino face,
thin lips, straight hair and long pointed nose, how odd I must
look.

What did blacks really think of whites? My main job as editor
of *Drum* was to try to see with African eyes; as I became more
immersed in the African world, I began to view my own race
from the outside. Europeans looked odd.

"You know, Tony, I don't think whites are really human,"
said Todd one day. As whites regard Africans as natives or
boys, not people or men[1], so Africans never describe whitemen
(which they spell, significantly, in one word) as *abantu*, or
people.[2] There is a large vocabulary of African words to describe
Europeans, including *abalumbi* (magicians), *izinjada* (wildcats),
and the Zulu phrase *abandlebe zikhanya ilanga*, meaning "those
whose ears reflect the sunlight".

I found Africans regarded Europeans as strange animals,
rather than perfect human beings, or standard-bearers of civilisation. The insults that white men throw on black men are
returned in good measure. Some whites think black men look
like animals: and vice-versa; the long hair and thin lips of a

[1]See, for example, two headlines in the *Rand Daily Mail*. "GUILTY OF ASSAULT
ON NATIVE: FINED £20." "ILL-TREATED ANIMALS: FINED £25." 19/7/52.
[2]It is a curious irony that by using the word "bantu" to describe Africans,
Europeans automatically exclude themselves from being called "people."

white man are at least as ape-like as the flat faces and dark skin of the black man.[1] We think they are materialistic: they think we are. "To the Bantu," says the distinguished African scholar, Selby Ngcobo, "the Europeans, probably because of their materialistic outlook, lack the essential quality of human beings, which is best conveyed by the Zulu word 'ubuntu'."[2]

Perhaps Africans still tend to regard whites partly as *abalumbi*, magicians; but then, to them we almost are. When Can Themba, a B.A. and senior teacher, joined our staff, he needed a new pass; he queued for two days at the Pass Office, and then asked me to go with him. "You see, you're *white*." Unwillingly I went. An unmoving queue curled round the building. Can beckoned me to a side entrance, SLEGS VIR BLANKES, and the serried ranks parted as if by a magic wand. Can pushed me to a white clerk; a fierce Zulu pushed blacks out of my way. "Make way for the baas!" No matter if I was a lunatic or a criminal, so long as I was white. The white clerk switched from scorn to a smile.

"Yes, sir, where's your boy?" Can came meekly forward, and was given a pass.

To most Africans, white men are enormously rich. The rudest word for a white man is *Igxagxa*, "poor white man": an *Igxagxa* is like a hen which doesn't lay eggs. White men are expected to have unlimited supplies of "white bread" to give out.

Can and I were talking one day about how blacks viewed whites.

"Whites are things to be used," he said; "they can be very useful if they're handled properly. But they're unpredictable, you never know where you are. You must get as much as you can out of them, obviously; and whatever you do, you must avoid annoying them. If they want to, they can wreck you...."

"Handling whites" is an important part of an African's education: a white man's whim can bring ruin, and by lifting a

[1] See Geoffrey Gorer: *Africa Dances*. (Lehman).
[2] G. H. Calpin (ed.): *The South African Way of Life*.

little finger he can transform your life. You must flatter him, study him, coax him, handle him with the greatest care, and at all costs avoid disfavour. By calling him "lord of the earth" or "everlasting king", you can probably earn a threepenny tip. It was, of course, characteristic of any subject race; I had seen it in post-war Germany, when the British became a temporary *Herrenvolk* who could make or break their German underlings.

The mock humility of Africans towards whites is usually successful, and the whites remain largely unaware of the deception. Like any master race, they like to sentimentalise their relations with their servants; they assume that insults or blows are quickly forgotten in benevolence, and that their paternalism is returned by gratitude. There is still much genuine goodwill and loyalty between white masters and black servants in Africa; but it is difficult to penetrate behind the barrier of duplicity. The most faithful Kikuyu servants in Kenya were often the most ruthless of the Mau Mau.

I learnt much about whites from talking with blacks: they saw and heard things that no white man could see. Whites, not caring what Africans said or thought, had few inhibitions or restraints in front of them; and African servants, still with the peasant's quick instinctive grasp of character, listened, observed, and deduced. No man was a hero to his "boy".

Sitting at the Back o' the Moon, I often overheard Africans telling stories about their white baasies. . . .

The favourite discussion was always about the English and the Afrikaners. Before the 1953 election, there were endless arguments about the Nationalist Party (predominantly Afrikaner) and the United Party (predominantly English). . . .

"There's no difference really, man; true's God! They both want the same thing: they both want apartheid! The English just use long words and big talk, isn't it? Segregation—ah, democracy—ah, civilised men. . . . The Dutchmen just say 'you blerry Kaffir, you, voetsak!' They both mean the same; but with the Dutchmen, you know where you are, man! Give me the Nats!"

"It's true! Those United Party boys are smart! Old Jannie Smuts—whew! When he thinks the Japs are going to invade us, he says 'Okay, boys, we're all together; we'll give you natives anything you want. . . . then we'll all fight the Japs, eh?' And then when the scare's over, he turns round and kicks us. Ag, he was smart—but he can't fool me, man!"

"Yes, man, with Danny Malan you know where you are. 'I'm going to keep the Kaffirs in their place,' he says to the Dutchmen, and he does. He means it. Police, guns, passes, prison. We know who we're fighting. But if things got bad with Slim Jannie Smuts, he'd get Congress along and shake hands and say, 'Good morning, Mr. Xuma,' and everyone said, 'Old Smuts is a good guy really!' And we'd forget all about apartheid and all the bad laws; I'm telling you!"

"It's quite surprising, you know," said Can to Arthur one morning, looking through *East Africa and Rhodesia*, "how these English guys talk about 'Africans' these days. Nothing about natives at all."

"Huh, they're crafty, you see," said Arthur; "they call you Africans and mister, but they still exploit you; that's the new imperialism. . . ."

"You know where you are with the Dutchman," is a proverb among Africans. And it is probably true that the African and the Afrikaner understand each other in a way that the Englishman understands neither.

On the first night of the film *Cry, the Beloved Country*, I watched the crowd surging round the African cinema, which was already full. Afrikaner police stood by with rifles at their side, handcuffs gleaming, and helmets like upturned buckets above their motionless faces. Suddenly, with no warning, they charged the crowd with the butt-ends of their rifles, shouting at the Africans, and hitting them out of the way. I watched in disgust; then I noticed to my surprise that the Africans were regarding the charge rather as a game: they ducked and skipped in front of the police, dodging the swinging rifles, and shouting jokes to the policemen.

It was a shock to find that both Africans and Afrikaners used violence as a language. It was the heritage of Africa, not yet subdued by cities and civilisation. African and Afrikaner both belong to Africa. The young Afrikaner policeman coming to Johannesburg from a platteland farm, where his family may have been cut off from civilisation since the Great Trek, was in a situation not very different from the Zulu coming from his reserve. Both were detribalised, uprooted, facing a strange town life. They spoke the same language—not only of kicks and swear words, but of sympathy and suffering.

"I tell you the whites that really annoy me," someone said one night at the Back o' the Moon. "The missionaries and liberals," pronouncing the syllables with mocking gentility.

"Thank goodness I don't owe anything to the missionaries," said another, who had been educated, subsidised and employed by missionaries.

"The missionaries are all right, really," said Todd; "but, shucks, we used to get mad at them!"

"You know the most popular professor with the boys at Fort Hare?" said Can. "He was a tough Afrikaner who used to walk into the classroom and say: 'Don't think for a moment that I'm doing this job because I *like* you Africans. I'm doing it because I'm *paid*.'"

"I wouldn't like to be a missionary," said Henry, "the natives are so ungrateful! Remember that mission school that was burnt down by the students? Eleven thousand pounds of damage!"

It is one of the great tragedies of Africa that the Europeans who work most for Africans, missionaries, liberals and welfare workers, bear the brunt of the bitterness between the races.

"I hate you liberals," someone said to me one night at the Back o' the Moon; "I can't hate the others because I don't meet them. . . ."

In the liberals' drawing-rooms, where Africans and Europeans sat uneasily together, one could see the full agony of race relations, and the rift that apartheid had cut. All the misunderstandings and misdirections from white to black showed up in the brief unhappy contact.

No Europeans in South Africa can escape the implications of white supremacy; the more confidence and satisfaction he gains from helping and befriending Africans, the more bitter becomes the African's dependence on a white man's favours. Of all the things that whites have taken from blacks, confidence has been the most valuable, and it is confidence that will be hardest to restore.

CHAPTER TWELVE

Dauntless One

The barrier of apartheid, and the rise of African Nationalism, pressed Africans towards the acceptance of a convenient and comforting rule, that all whites were bad, and all blacks were good. The white *baas*, this strong and simple enemy, explained all troubles and hardships, all mediocrity and shortcomings. But, however much Africans grumbled about whites, most of all whites who were trying to do good, there was always one strange exception, whose existence was of incalculable importance—Father Trevor Huddleston.

Huddleston was so inextricably a part of black South Africa, so much the fixed star against which all other liberal activities were judged, that it is difficult now that he has been recalled to imagine South Africa without him. Even in our very secular and practical task of publishing *Drum*, we came immediately into contact with Huddleston. In the first place, seven out of our African staff of twenty came from St. Peter's School in Johannesburg, of which Huddleston was superintendent.

"Huddleston was never too busy to listen to a student's sorrows and ambitions—especially ambitions," said Arthur.

"I once heckled him at a meeting," said Can. "He asked me to come round and talk it over afterwards. He's the sort of guy you can *argue* with."

"He's the only white man who could safely walk through locations alone at night—except the police," said Arthur.

"I wish he was black," said Benson, our African Nationalist.

Trevor Huddleston first came to South Africa in 1943, to be

priest-in-charge of the mission of the Community of the Resurrection in Sophiatown. He came from a religious family: an ancestor, Father John Huddleston, was the Restoration priest who received Charles II back into the Church. Trevor's father, Sir Ernest Huddleston, was a Director of the Royal Indian Marine.

Huddleston first became interested in missionary work during vacations from Oxford, spent with the hop-pickers in Kent. Soon after leaving Oxford, he became a novice in the Community of the Resurrection, a monastic community within the Church of England, which aimed to reproduce the life of the early Christians recorded in the Acts of the Apostles. "Not one of them said that aught of the things which he possessed was his own; but they had all things in common." He took the three oaths of poverty, chastity and obedience.

Meeting Huddleston at a Johannesburg cocktail party, with his warm social ease, his feeling for people and his gentle tolerance, it was difficult to imagine him against the austere and rigid background of a Yorkshire monastery preoccupied with the business of prayer. Huddleston's public life seemed so practical and comprehensible, so much what others would wish to have done if they had the courage and the strength, that it was hard to realise that his political activity in Africa was merely an extension of an unworldly monastic life beyond the comprehension of most laymen, in which prayer and eternity loomed far larger than political meetings and feeding-schemes.

"It may seem odd," Huddleston once said to me, "but one of the most wonderful things about the Community to me is the *freedom*. Within those three vows, I can do or say or write anything, provided it does not offend other members. That's why I say so much."

Huddleston spent six years in Sophiatown. "That was the happiest time of my life," he said. When I stayed in Sophiatown, I found his name was still a legend. They called him "die

Jerry", because of his close-cropped German-looking hair; his tall cassocked figure strode through the township, surrounded by African parishioners. He wandered into the cinema, listened to meetings, joined a bread queue in the early morning. He started a cocoa club for young *tsotsis*, and enrolled them as servers in the church. Someone pointed out to me the spot where he had walked between two *tsotsis* fighting with knives. Everyone knew Huddleston's name in Sophiatown. I saw his photograph stuck on the wall of a tiny backyard shack.

From Sophiatown, he was transferred to Rosettenville, in Johannesburg. He was appointed Provincial of his Community in South Africa.

I first met Trevor Huddleston when he asked us if we had a job for Arthur. I waited to see him in his small cell at Rosettenville. I looked around at the photographs of ex-St. Peter's boys, the theological volumes, the *Church Times*, and *Drum*. The cell was his sitting-room, classroom, office and study.

Huddleston came in, a tall, dignified figure, wearing his long black cassock, with a worn leather belt round his waist, and a cross dangling from one side. He had a long face with a deep chin, greying, close-cropped hair, and direct eyes. He spoke with a simple directness, as if Arthur and *Drum* were all that he had ever thought about.

In the next three years I saw him in many different roles. I saw him at African functions and Congress gatherings, at European cocktail parties and fund-raising meetings. All roads seemed to lead to Huddleston. I went to the funeral of Oubaas, to find him conducting the burial service. When one of our staff who was unhappy in *Drum* found other work, I found that it had been arranged by Huddleston. Many of the best members of our staff were sent to us by him; two of them he sent after they had been expelled from St. Peter's.

When Huddleston raised funds for a swimming-pool to be built at Orlando, Todd composed a chorale in his praise, called

Makhalipile, the dauntless one. Huddleston invited me to hear it being recorded by the St. Peter's choir, with Todd at the piano:

> Makhalipile, please pass this way.
> Makhalipile, please come and save us,
> Your children are hungry!

(Makhalipile, explains Todd, was a bold warrior of an un-known tribe, who was adopted by another people, whose leaders were lost or captured.)

> Well, tell us now Makhalipile: you must be
> A very strange creature-man. You could be in
> Florida, Riviera, India, Brazil too! But here
> you are, in Africa!
> Well, folks, let's eat him up! Let's fry him
> Up! Let's eat him up!
> No, no!
> Why?
> He's not fat enough! . . .

(This is a skit, says Todd, on those people who say that the African is a backward, helpless savage. No good can ever come of him. Nobody should waste his time on them. Didn't they devour the missionaries in the early days? . . .)

With his warm, strong personality, Huddleston spanned the gulf between black and white. His close personal friendships were irrespective of colour. He dined with Sir Ernest Oppenheimer, and stayed with Sir Evelyn Baring. He was a close friend of Oliver Tambo, Secretary of the African Congress, and Yusuf Cachalia, Secretary of the Indian Congress. Most distinguished visitors to South Africa seemed to find their way, somehow or other, to Huddleston's cell.

133

He never thought it odd that he should get mixed up in politics. When someone accused him of being an agitator, he replied: "The Christian is always, if he is true to his calling, an agitator. . . ." He was determined to resist the pressure of white society and white supremacy. He preached a sermon at Christ the King in Sophiatown, on the text: "He that loseth his life for my sake shall find it." "It reminds us," he said, "that at the heart of our religion there lies a principle in absolute contradiction to the principles by which the world speaks and thinks and acts. . . ." Abiding by this principle, Huddleston inevitably became caught up in African politics.

Many of Huddleston's African friends were in Congress and they often sought his advice and support; and in his opposition to government legislation, he found himself on the same platform as Congress. With the outbreak of the defiance campaign he was, like other liberal whites, perplexed by the dilemma of defiance. Could he give his support to the deliberate breaking of laws? Could he sit on the same platform with people with views very different from his own, including Marxists and Nationalists? Was passive resistance a legitimate means of protest?

Huddleston gave his answer at a meeting in February, 1953, called in protest against the new acts to suppress the defiance campaign. He spoke in front of nine hundred Congress delegates at the Trades Hall, Johannesburg—a solitary white figure facing a sea of black faces. He spoke in short simple phrases, pausing at the end of each for the Zulu interpreter.

"It has been the teaching of the Church through the centuries . . . that when government degenerates into tyranny. . . . laws cease to be binding upon its subjects." He concluded: "The future of South Africa is in *your* hands, that is certain. . . . I pray God he may give you strength. . . . I identify myself entirely with your struggle."[1]

[1] *Rand Daily Mail*. 16/2/53.

"I've been trying to pluck up courage to say that for months," he said to me, as he hurried out of the hall on his way to a service. "I'm glad I've taken the plunge."

Some time later, he showed me a copy of an English news letter. Under the heading of "Dangerous Men", it said: "Huddleston is either the dupe of Communists, or worse, he may know what he is doing."

"I'm wondering whether it's worth suing him," said Huddleston. "I'm convinced that Communism is not a serious danger in South Africa," he said, "otherwise I wouldn't be doing what I am. . . . It'll be a terrible thing if I'm wrong."

Huddleston's identification with Congress made him one of the government's marked men. They blamed him for any African opposition. "In the middle ages," said Mr. de Klerk, Strijdom's brother-in-law and Minister of Lands, "people like Michael Scott and Huddleston would have been burned at the stake. . . ."

The police began following Huddleston, meeting him at airports, waiting outside houses which he visited, searching the rooms of his hosts. They raided Congress meetings and took names of everyone present as they filed out; they sent police cameramen to photograph the audience row by row.

"They seem to be closing in," said Huddleston one day when I went to see him. "I find it difficult to get a platform now. People are scared by the police, and I can't blame them: they politely cancel their invitations to speak. It's hard enough getting somewhere to exhibit photographs."

"People say I'm a politician," he said to me one afternoon, sitting in a classroom at St. Peter's writing out passes for his schoolboys to go into town, so that they should not be arrested. "But all I'm interested in, really, is people: particularly these people," waving at the queue of schoolboys.

St. Peter's was Huddleston's great pride. It was known as the "Black Eton of South Africa", and its distinguished alumni included Peter Abrahams, Todd, and Oliver Tambo, acting Secretary of Congress. St. Peter's added an English liberal education to the tough schooling of a townee African, to produce a kind of cultured cockney.

Huddleston was interested in every side of the school and schoolboys. "Anthony, when are you going to take some pictures of our jazz band?" he asked. "Jake Tuli's giving a boxing demonstration next week. . . ." "I've arranged a debate between a white school and St. Peter's." "You might like to do a feature about our printing press: Lady Oppenheimer has just given us some Perpetua. . . ."

But St. Peter's was doomed.

The Bantu Education Act of 1954 enabled the government to take over mission schools. In place of European education, a new type of "Bantu Education" would be provided, more suited to the African in the new South Africa.

The theory of "Bantu Education" had support from many Europeans including liberals; it took to extremes the "cultural apartheid" which had been inherent in the early numbers of *Drum*. The idea that Africans should "develop along their own lines" in the reserves, with their own culture and education, rather than ape the white man on the fringes of the cities, appealed to many fair-minded Europeans. There was a case for a more realistic education, less tied to book-learning and European traditions.

But the basis of Bantu[1] Education was apartheid. "Bantu education means slave education," said the African National Congress. "It was designed to create cheap and docile labour for the mines, farms and other similar industries." Congress at first planned to boycott the new education, but later postponed action till an alternative schooling could be provided. However,

[1] The very word Bantu, now in favour with the Government, is objectionable to many Africans, with its tribal associations: "Flora, fauna and bantu," as one African said to me.

when the schools were taken over by the government in April, 1955, six thousand children boycotted the new education. Dr. Verwoerd retaliated by dismissing the teachers involved, and excluding the children from school in the future, though later he partially relented.

Trevor Huddleston, with other missionaries, was faced with a dilemma by the Bantu Education Act. Should St. Peter's continue under the new régime, teaching a syllabus which it considered un-Christian, or should it close down? Was Bantu Education better than no education? The Anglican bishops in South Africa, excepting the Bishop of Johannesburg, agreed to lease their mission school buildings to the government. "The alternative," they said, "would throw many teachers out of employment, and leave many children without opportunity of any kind of instruction."

But Huddleston refused to compromise in any way with the Bantu Education Act.

"It is still happily possible to prefer death to dishonour," he said. "St. Peter's will die. . . ."

In an article explaining the Act, he wrote:

"There is only one path open to the African: it is the path back to tribal culture and tradition: to ethnic groups; to the reserves; to anywhere other than the privileged places habited by the master race. It is because we cannot accept such principles that we are closing St. Peter's. . . .

"It has been a decision made in anguish and only after the most careful thought and prayer. For it means the end of forty years of labour and devotion, and it means the break-up of a tradition of which we are unashamedly proud."

"In weeping for St. Peter's," wrote Peter Abrahams about his old school, "I weep for a new generation of slum kids for whom there will be no escape, as there was for me, through St. Peter's."

Six months after the introduction of Bantu Education, when St. Peter's was doomed, mission buildings were threatened with removal, and his beloved Sophiatown was being razed to the ground, it was announced that Father Huddleston was to be recalled to be Master of the Novices in the monkish seclusion of his community in Yorkshire.

It was impossible for the Africans, with whom he had become so deeply and steadily involved, to understand this sudden recall to prayer and teaching—to weigh the certainty of his present achievement against the spiritual future of his community, or to see South Africa as only one frontier of a broader fight. What can South Africa be like without Trevor Huddleston? Perhaps this demanding yet stimulating crisis of the races will throw up another great figure, as Huddleston in some ways succeeded Raymond Raynes and Michael Scott. Perhaps some whites, in their anxiety for a symbol, or a saint, exaggerate the importance of a single personality in a situation involving millions. But it is among Africans that all workers for Africans should be judged; and it will not be easy for them to find another white man who combines the firmness and conviction of a monk with the warm affection of a close friend.

CHAPTER THIRTEEN

Naked Man

The two bills of 1953 designed to suppress the defiance campaign made life difficult for Mr. Drum. Their powers were so wide that editors could be flogged for publishing any article "calculated to cause any person to commit an offence by way of protest".

"Mr. Drum, why don't you write about jails?" readers kept on asking.

Nearly a quarter of a million[1] people go to jail every year in South Africa, out of a total population of twelve million; the great majority are Africans. Most Africans go to jail during their lifetime—usually for petty statutory offences such as being without a pass or permit.

During the defiance campaign, when eight thousand people deliberately went to jail, we heard many stories of beatings, bad food, filthy cells, and a humiliating "tausa dance" which prisoners performed naked when they were searched for tobacco.

"You'll never get the jails changed," a liberal friend told me. "I've been trying to get penal reform for years. Beating and kicking is part of the prison tradition: it's the only way that they can make non-European prisons worse than life outside."

Jim and I were determined that *Drum* should investigate jails. But no article could be effective without photographs, which were our main weapon; and to photograph the inside of a jail seemed impossible. All prisoners were stripped and searched on

[1] In 1951, the last year on record, 245,950 people were sent to jail.

entering jail; and no warder would be foolish enough to take photographs for us.

I toured round the Reef jails with Bob Gosani—Germiston, Boksburg, Leeuwkop, Pretoria. We searched for peep-holes, hideouts and overlooking buildings; but everywhere there were high walls with barred windows.

We walked round "the Fort"—the big jail on a hill above Johannesburg: "Number Four", as the Africans call it, is the most hated and overcrowded of all the jails in South Africa.[1] It has a grim castellated main gate, a relic from its days as a fort in the Boer War, and a high bank all round. At four o'clock crocodiles of African prisoners came in from work, and the gates clanged open and shut.

Round the side of the fort was a narrow passage; we could see, through cracks in the corrugated iron, the courtyard where prisoners were paraded, with the cells behind.

On the other side of the passage there was a flat-roofed building, high enough to overlook the jail. It was a white nurses' home for the hospital. When I came back to the office I rang up the superintendent, and asked permission to photograph views of Johannesburg from the roof.

Bob borrowed a powerful telescopic camera, which looked like a cannon and needed two people to carry it.

We made a plan. I could not send Bob alone to take photographs—African photographers were unheard of. I asked my secretary, Deborah Duncan, who was Pat's sister, to go with him: officially, she would be the photographer, and Bob and Arthur would be "boys".

We rehearsed in the office. Deborah bossed round Bob and Arthur.

"Boy, lift that over there; come on, boy, get on with it!"

[1] In 1951, the average daily non-European population of Johannesburg Central jail was 1,944, against an authorised capacity of 979, according to figures supplied by the Minister of Justice (House of Assembly, 7/3/52).

Bob and Arthur said: "Yes, madam. No, madam. Does the missus want it here?"

Just before four, they drove to the nurses' home. The superintendent led them to the roof.

"What a glorious view!" said Deborah, looking down the side away from the jail, and focusing her small camera.

"We've even got the jail on the other side," said the superintendent.

Deborah looked down. Only fifty feet below was the prison courtyard. The prisoners had just come back from work, and had squatted four deep across the yard jammed against each other. At one end a European warder in shirt-sleeves was standing with his hands on his hips. In front of the warder stood a prisoner, stripped naked.

Suddenly the naked man jumped up in the air like a frisky monkey, clapped his hands above him, opened his mouth wide and turned round in mid-air, so that he landed with his back to the warder. Then he bent down with his arms stretched out, while the warder watched him intently. The naked man looked round at the warder, who nodded; he picked up his clothes from the ground, and walked off to the cells. The next man in the queue, by now stripped naked, ran up to the warder and repeated the routine.

This was the "tausa dance" which we had heard about. Bob and Arthur quickly assembled the cannon. Deborah returned to the other side of the roof, and took pictures of the criss-cross streets of Johannesburg. She talked to the superintendent about the flowers on the roof-garden.

Bob pointed the cannon at the tausa dancer, and clicked. The prisoners waiting crouched on the ground noticed this odd shape being pointed at them and giggled. The warder at first was too absorbed in watching the naked men to notice; but then he looked up and saw the camera. Another warder arrived, and they began to stare threateningly at the roof. Deborah and

Bob hastily packed up. Bob went back to the dark-room and developed the picture.

What a story there was in that one photograph. The thin, taut, naked black figure, with his head shaved bare, looked like a huge leaping frog. Beside him stood the white warder. Behind was a mass of black faces, arms and legs; the younger ones smiled at the joke of being photographed in their debasement. The long-term prisoners, in their white caps, looked beyond laughter.

*   *   *

In the meantime I had received an article called "My Time in Jail" from Manilal Gandhi. Manilal had just served a sentence of fifty days in Germiston jail, as a result of "defying" with Patrick Duncan. He was disgusted by the prison conditions, and asked us if we could find room for his article.

"Prisoners are not only shouted at, but beaten up, knocked, clapped, charged by African warders with sticks, and by the white warders with batons," wrote Manilal. "If any prisoner has a complaint against a warder, he seldom gets a proper hearing. . . . I was horrified to see an African warder strike three African prisoners on their heads with a stick, making their heads bleed, just because unknowingly they were standing in the wrong queue. . . . My blankets were ridden with lice, and the food was dirty. . . . African prisoners were treated like beasts."

We decided to publish Manilal's article in our next issue as a prelude to our own investigation.

The day after the article appeared, the *Rand Daily Mail* quoted from it, under the heading PRISONERS BEATEN UP, KNOCKED, KICKED, SLAPPED. The Johannesburg *Star* followed with a denial by a visiting magistrate of Germiston jail.

"I have seen no signs of such maltreatment," he said. "In all the time I have been here, I have only had two complaints. . . ."

The Director of Prisons, Mr. V. R. Verster, joined in. "The allegations are completely unfounded. Mr. Gandhi, who took part in the defiance campaign, is not an unbiased observer."

The argument continued in the newspapers for a fortnight.

"I substantiate the statements made by Mr. Gandhi. They are nothing but the truth," said Yusuf Cachalia, who had been to jail during the Durban passive resistance campaign.

"I have never encountered a solitary circumstance to support Mr. Gandhi's charges," said a Germiston prison visitor.

"Non-European prisoners are taught the prison regulations by blows and other forms of assault," said an ex-warder.

"I am not prepared to believe recent allegations of ill-treatment in non-European jails," said Mr. Swart, the Minister of Justice. "It is strange that all these complaints come from defiance campaign prisoners. . . ."

All the magistrates, visitors and officials denied Gandhi's allegations; everyone who had been to jail supported them. The reason for the discrepancy was obvious: prisoners dared not complain for fear of reprisals, and the warders always behaved themselves when the visitors came.

Meanwhile, we were discussing *Drum*'s investigation. With a quarter of a million Africans going to jail every year, there was plenty of evidence; but we had to be certain of our facts and details. I wanted to concentrate attention on one jail, the Fort.

"The real story we want," I said, "is *Mr. Drum Goes to Jail*."

"I'll go to jail if you like," said Benson.

"No," said Henry. "I'll go. I'm Mr. Drum."

"Do you think you can get inside?"

"That's easy," said Henry. "My difficulty has always been to stay outside."

There was a snag. The new "public safety act" of 1953 made it a serious offence for anyone to defy the law, or to encourage defiance.

I rang up a solicitor friend.

"Can you tell me the safest way of getting an African to jail for a week, without defying the law?"

"Look here, Anthony, my job is getting people out of jail, not putting them in. I can't possibly advise you how to break the law. It's most improper."

I went to see another solicitor, who was fascinated by my problem.

"Let me see. . . . 'Calculated to cause any person to commit an offence by way of protest.' Of course, that can be given a broad interpretation; but I think that, provided your reporter is arrested in an inconspicuous fashion, without setting an example to others; and provided that he can show later that his purpose was *bona fide* to investigate prisons, he should be quite safe—as far as anyone is safe. But you should not, I think, give him any definite *order* to get arrested," he added, with a smile.

I said to Henry: "Go away and enjoy yourself. If by any chance you get arrested, I'd be interested to hear about it."

"I'm always ending up in jail, anyway," said Henry, and went off.

Henry decided to visit a friend in Boksburg location, without a permit. He arranged for someone to tell the police. He was taken to the police station.

"Ag! Don't be silly, man! Go away and don't do it again," they said, and Henry went sheepishly home.

Next day he boarded a train to Orlando without a ticket; the ticket collector came round, and he refused to pay the fare of 1s. 8d. The railway policeman at Orlando station was genial.

"Look here," he said. "Just go up to the first person you see, and ask him to lend you the money."

"No," said Henry stubbornly. He was arrested, and spent the night in the police station.

"You'll spend Christmas in Number Four, I promise you, you blerry Kaffir," said an angry railway policeman.

Henry came up before the magistrate next morning, but the policeman who had arrested Henry couldn't be found.

"I'd like a remand, sir," said the prosecutor.

"No. Case dismissed," said the magistrate.

Henry slunk away.

He tried again. He put a bottle of brandy in his hip pocket, and walked jauntily up and down outside Marshall Square, the police headquarters in Johannesburg. No one took any notice. He followed policemen about, singing and shouting. They showed no interest. He started drinking the bottle of brandy, in front of Marshall Square. Nobody stopped him. He got drunk, and became involved in a brawl. They arrested him, and took him inside to the cells.

Henry came up before the magistrate in the drunks' court next morning. He noticed that the court interpreter was a friend of his.

"Charge—drunkenness. Anything to say?"

"Nothing, baas."

"Five days or ten shillings."

Just as he was about to go down rejoicing into the cells, the court interpreter came up.

"It's all right, Henry, I've paid your fine, you're free."

Henry returned to the office in despair.

"Shucks, if it was somebody else who couldn't get arrested, I could understand, Hen; but you!" said Todd. "What's wrong with the cops?"

Henry tried again. He walked about Johannesburg late at night after curfew without a permit. He hovered around every street corner where there was a policeman. At the corner of Rissik Street and Plein Street, a white policeman demanded his permit.

"I haven't got one, meneer." (It always annoys an Afrikaans policeman to be called meneer—mister—and not baas.) The policeman looked him up and down; he turned to the black policeman beside him.

"Well, what shall I do, George? Do you want to arrest him?"

"Ja, baas," said the African policeman eagerly, anxious to impress the baas. Henry was arrested and taken, once more, to Marshall Square.

Next morning I had a phone call from an African who worked at the courts.

"Sir, I've got a message from one of your staff, Mr. Nxumalo. He says there's been an unfortunate accident. He was arrested last night after curfew, and he's just been sentenced to five days in the Fort. So he won't be able to come to work today."

CHAPTER FOURTEEN

Mr. Drum Goes to Jail

This was Henry's story:

We were taken to Johannesburg Central Prison by truck. We arrived at the prison immediately after one o'clock. From the truck we were given orders to "shayisa" (close up), fall in twos and "sharp shoot" (run) to the prison reception office. From then on "Come on, Kaffir!" was the operative phrase from both black and white prison officials, and in all languages.

Many of us who were going to prison for the first time didn't know exactly where the reception office was. Although the prison officials were with us, no one was directing us. But if a prisoner hesitated, slackened his half-running pace and looked round, he got a hard boot kick on the buttocks, a slap on his face or a whipping from the warders. Fortunately there were some second offenders with us who knew where to go. We followed them through the prison's many zig-zagging corridors until we reached the reception office.

The reception office had a terrifyingly brutal atmosphere. It was full of foul language. A number of khaki-uniformed white officials stood behind a long cement bar-like curved counter. They wore the initials "P.S.G.D." on their shoulders. When they were not joking about prisoners they were swearing at them and taking down their particulars. Two were taking fingerprints and hitting the prisoners in the face when they made mistakes.

Five long-term prisoners attended to us. One came up to me and said he knew me. I didn't know him. He asked for cigarettes, but I didn't have any. Another told us to take off our watches and money and hold them in our hands. These were to be kept separate from our other possessions. Another asked me for 2s. 6d.; but I had 5d. only and he wasn't interested. He noticed I had a copy of *Time* magazine in my hand and asked for it. I gave it to him. He hid it under the counter so that the warders couldn't see it. Later he asked me what paper it was, how old it was and whether it was interesting. After we had undressed, one long-term prisoner demanded my fountain pen.

"That's a fine pen you've got, eh?" he asked. "How about giving it to me?"

I said: "I'm afraid I can't; it's not my pen, it's my boss's pen."

"Hi, don't tell me lies, you bastard," he said. "What the hell are you doing with your boss's pen in prison? Did you steal it?" he asked.

I said I hadn't stolen it. I was using it and had it in my possession when I was arrested.

"Give it here. I want it for my work here; if you refuse you'll see blood streaming down your dirty mouth soon." I was nervous, but didn't reply.

"Look, you little fool, I'll see that you are well treated in prison if you give me that pen."

The other prisoners looked at me anxiously. I didn't know whether they approved of my giving my pen or not; but their anxious look seemed to suggest that their fate in prison lay in that pen. I gave it away.

We were called up to have our fingerprints taken by a white warder. Before taking the impression the warder made a loud complaint that the hand glove he used when taking impressions was missing. He swore at the long-term prisoner who assisted him and told him to find it. The other white prison officials helped him find the glove. He was a stout, middle-aged man, apparently a senior official. He took my impression, examined it and then complained that my hands were wet. He hit me on the mouth with the back of his gloved hand. I rubbed my right thumb on my hair and he took another impression.

From there I ran down to the end of the wide curved desk to have my height taken, and stood beside the measuring rod, naked. A long-term prisoner took my height. When finished with a prisoner, he would throw his ticket on the floor for the prisoner to pick up.

We were then taken to the showers in another room. There was neither soap nor a towel. After a few minutes under water we were told to get out, and skip to get dry. Then our prison clothes were thrown at us—a red shirt and a torn white pair of short pants. They looked clean; but the side cap and the white jacket which were issued to me later were filthy. The jacket had dry sweat on the neck.

From then on we were barefoot, and were marched to the hospital for medical examination in double time. Another long-term prisoner lined us up, ordered us to undress and turn our faces to the wall, so that we would not pollute the medical officer with our breath when he came to examine us.

After this we were marched down to the main court of the prison in double time. Here we found different white and black warders and long-term prisoners, who took charge of us. Again we undressed and had our second shower in thirty minutes. I was unable to make out my own clothes after the shower and the skipping. The African warder kicked me in the stomach with the toe of his boot. I tried to hold the boot to protect myself, and fell on my face. He asked if I had had an operation to my stomach. I said no. He looked at me scornfully. I got up, picked up the clothes in front of me and ran to join the others squatting on the floor.

After another rollcall we were marched to the top of the court to collect our food. The dishes were lined in rows and each prisoner picked up the dish nearest to him. The zinc dishes containing the food were rusty. The top of my dish was broken in three places. The food itself was boiled whole mealies with fat. We were marched to No. 7 cell, given blankets and a sleeping-mat and locked in. We ate. The time was about 4.30 p.m. Clean water and toilet buckets were installed, but the water wasn't enough for sixty people. The long-term prisoners warned us not to use the water as if we were at our own homes. An old man went to fetch water with his dish at one stage and the long-term prisoner in charge of the cell swore at him. The old man insisted that he was thirsty and continued scooping the water. The long-term prisoner took the water away from him and threw it all over the old man's face.

There was a stinking smell when prisoners used the toilet bucket at night without toilet paper. At 8 p.m. the bell rang and we were ordered to be quiet and sleep. Some prisoners who had smuggled *dagga* and matches into the cell started conversing in whispers, and smoking. The blankets were full of bugs; I turned round and round during the night without being able to sleep, and kept my prison clothes on for protection against bugs.

We were up at about six o'clock the following morning. I tried to get some water to wash my dish and drink. The dish was full of the previous night's fat, and I didn't know how I was going to do it. But the long-term prisoner shouted at me and ordered me to leave the water alone. I obeyed. He swore at me in Afrikaans, and ordered me to wipe the urine which was overflowing from the toilet bucket with a small sack cloth. I did so. He said I must wipe it dry; but the cloth was so small that the floor remained wet.

He told me to find two other prisoners to help me carry the toilet bucket out, empty it and clean it. It was full of the night's excrement. There were no volunteers, so I slipped to a corner and waited. He saw me and rushed at me.

"What did I tell you, damn it, what did I say?" He slapped me on the left cheek with his open right hand as he spoke. He said he could have me put in solitary confinement if he wished. He could tell the chief warder that I had messed the floor and I would get an additional punishment. I kept quiet. I had done nothing of the sort. Finally he ordered two other prisoners to help me.

We emptied the bucket and washed it as the other prisoners were being lined up in readiness for breakfast. One of my colleagues tried to wash his hands after we had emptied the bucket. The white warder saw him and slashed him with the strap part of his baton. The dish containing my porridge—and many others—still had the previous night's fat. It had been washed in cold water. The breakfast itself was yellow porridge with half-cooked pieces of turnips, potatoes, carrots and other vegetables I could not recognise. No spoons are provided; so I had my breakfast with my stinking soiled hands. I didn't feel like eating, but feared that I would be inviting further trouble.

After breakfast we were divided into many work "spans" (parties). I spent my first day with a span cutting grass, pulling out weeds with my hands and pushing wheelbarrows at the Johannesburg Teachers' Training College in Parktown. We walked for about half a mile to our place of work, and I was one of two prisoners carrying a heavy, steel food can, which contained lunch porridge for a party of sixteen. Two warders escorted us: one white and one black. Once I slackened because we were going down a precipice: my fingers were sore and the burden was heavy. The old white warder who was carrying a big rifle slashed me on my bare legs with the strap of his baton.

We returned to jail at four. We were ordered to undress and "tausa," a common routine of undressing prisoners when they return from work, searching their clothes, their mouths, armpits, and rectum for hidden articles. I didn't know how it was done. I opened my mouth, turned round and didn't jump and clap my hands. The white warder conducting the search hit me with

151

his fist on my left jaw, threw my clothes at me and went on searching the others. I ran off, and joined the food queue.

One night I didn't have a mat to sleep on. Long-term prisoners in charge of the cells sometimes took a bundle of mats to make themselves comfortable beds, to the discomfort of other prisoners. In practice, a prisoner never knows where he will sleep next day. It is all determined by your speed in "tausa", food and blanket queues. A prisoner uses another prisoner's dirty blankets every night.

In the four days I was in prison—I got a remission of one day—I was kicked or thrashed every day. I saw many other prisoners being thrashed daily. I was never told what was expected of me, but had to guess. Sometimes I guessed wrong and got into trouble.

Long-term and short-term prisoners mixed freely in the prison. For example, the famous Tiger, of Alexandra township, who was doing a ten-year sentence for various crimes, was one of the most important persons in prison during my time. He was responsible for the in and out movements of other prisoners and warders. Though I was a short-term prisoner, I, too, took orders from Tiger.

It was a common practice for short-term prisoners to give their small piece of meat to long-term prisoners on meat days for small favours such as tobacco, *dagga*, shoes (which are supposed to be supplied to Coloured prisoners only), wooden spoons—or to ensure that they were always supplied with sleeping-mats.

Thrashing time for warders was roll call, breakfast time and supper time. For long-term prisoners it was inside the cells at all times. Long-term prisoners thrashed prisoners more severely and more often than the prison officials themselves, and often in the presence of either white or black warders.

On the day of our discharge we were marched to the reception office for our personal effects and checking out. The long-term prisoners officiating there told us not to think that we were already out of prison. They kicked and slapped prisoners for the slightest mistake, and sometimes for no mistake at all; and promised them additional sentences if they complained. In the office there was a notice warning prisoners to see that their personal belongings were recorded in the prison's book correctly, and exactly as they had brought them. But I dared not complain about my pen which was commandeered on my arrival, lest I be detained. The prisoner who took it pretended not to know me.

Before we left the prison we were told the superintendent would address us. We could make complaints to him if we had any. But the fat Zulu warder who paraded us to the yard for the superintendent's inspection said we must tell him everything was all right if we wanted to leave prison.

"This is a court of law," he said; "you are about to go home, but before you leave this prison the big boss of the prison will address you. He will ask you if you have any complaints. Now I take it that you all want to go to your homes—to your wives and children—you don't want to stay here. So if the big boss asks you if everything is all right, say: 'Yes, sir.' If he says have you any complaints say: 'No, sir.' You hear?"

In a chorus we said "Yes."

Just then one prisoner complained that his Kliptown train ticket was missing from his things. It was a season ticket. The Zulu warder pulled him aside and said:

"You think you're clever, eh? You'll see!" He put him at the tail-end of the parade. The superintendent came and we answered him as instructed. Most of us were seeing him for the first time. The Zulu warder said nothing about the complaint of the man from Kliptown. Later, as we were going to collect our monies from the pay office, the man from Kliptown was escorted to the reception office to see C., the famous fierce discharge officer. C. said the man's papers showed that he was charged at Fordsburg and not at Kliptown. He was not entitled to any ticket. But the man insisted that he was arrested at Kliptown, charged at Fordsburg and appeared in Johannesburg. The fat Zulu warder said in broken Afrikaans:

"He's mad, sir."

He gave the man a hard slap in the face with his open hand, and said:

"You're just wasting the boss's time, eh? On your way. . . . voetsak!" And the man sneaked out.

One by one we zig-zagged our way out of the prison's many doors and gates and lined up in twos in front of the main and final gate. We were ordered to leave prison quietly and in pairs when the small gate was open. If we blocked the gate we would be thrashed. We were to come out in the order of the line. The man on the left would go out first and the one on the right would follow. The gate was opened. We saw freedom and blocked the gate in our anxiety. If they thrashed us we couldn't feel it. . . . we didn't look back!

*   *   *

I took Henry's story to our solicitor.

"It's risky, of course, but you can't avoid risks. If I were the editor, I'd use it."

For our third birthday number, in March, 1954, we published Henry's story, "Mr. Drum Goes to Jail." Underneath the photograph of the tausa dance we printed an extract from the prison regulations:

"The searching of a convict shall be conducted with due regard to decency and self-respect, and in as seemly a manner as is consistent with the necessity of discovering any concealed article."

The number appeared just as the controversy over Gandhi's article was dying down. The next day, the *Rand Daily Mail* republished the "tausa" picture, with part of Henry's story. There were no more denials.

Few people guessed how we took the pictures. A writer in the *Natal Sunday Tribune*, attacking the *Drum* article, said: "The very fact that the reporter from the *Drum* managed to smuggle a camera into prison, or was party to it, shows that from the outset he was contravening prison regulations."

"They used a helicopter." "They bribed one of the warders." "The whole thing was faked. . . ." I was introduced by a missionary as "the man who went to jail with a miniature camera." We never disclosed our prosaic methods.

"Now you're *asking* for trouble," said a newspaper editor after our article appeared. "You'll have the C.I.D. round immediately." "Have *they* come to see you yet?" I was asked every day in the pub. "There's a man in uniform outside, waiting to see you," said our solicitor at a party. "Seriously—has no one come yet?"

Two weeks later, a man came into the office and asked shyly:

"Can I speak to—er—Mr. Drum?"

"Well, I'm the editor. Can I help you?" I asked.

"Well, sir, I'm from the C.I.D. It's about this article 'Mr. Drum Goes to Jail.' "

"Yes?"

"Have you got a copy of the original photograph, which I could have?"

I fished out a copy waiting in the drawer. "Might I ask what you want it for?"

"We want it as evidence. We're bringing a case against the warder for contravening prison regulations."

I sank back in relief. I'd escaped the lashes. We checked quickly, and found that the warder had already been transferred to a junior post. Soon after, we heard rumours that the jails had improved since our article. Henry interviewed some prisoners coming out of jail.

"Since the third week in February there has been a vast improvement in prison conditions," said Joseph Hlope, who had finished a three months' sentence. "Warders are no longer assaulting prisoners indiscriminately. Long-term prisoners no longer kick and slap other prisoners at will. . . . Prisoners now get enough water to wash in the mornings. . . . All prisoners are issued with small pieces of paper for toilet use regularly. . . . Dancing round and clapping hands in the old 'tausa' style has been stopped. . . . Prisoners are no longer assaulted in the search queues."

The results of our jail article confirmed what we suspected, that the government was still sensitive to informed criticism.

The Orlando *tsotsis* gave a party for Henry.

"Jeez, Mr. Drum, that was a good job: cleaning up Number Four for us."

CHAPTER FIFTEEN

Off Whites

After "Mr. Drum Goes to Jail," our circulation in South Africa rose to seventy thousand. Our sales outside South Africa, mostly in West Africa, mounted to thirty thousand. The dream of a black magazine for Africa was beginning to come true.

"Should *Drum* be for Africans only?" We asked the question increasingly. There was a danger that, in our anxiety to be genuinely African, *Drum* would appear racialist. Could we extend our readership to other races, without losing the confidence of Africans? An inter-racial *Drum*, if it could be achieved, would increase both our circulation and our stature: a magazine read by all races could have a great power for good. But in an apartheid country the task was difficult.

Coloured readers seemed the next obvious target; the million people of mixed blood in South Africa had no important paper of their own, and they were more literate and well paid than the average African. But although, or because, many of them had African blood, their prejudice against Africans was often fiercer than the Europeans'. Could we persuade Coloureds to read the *Drum*? Would Africans resent pictures of Coloureds? We discussed the question constantly at editorial meetings.

"You must be careful, you see," said Job Rathebe; "we want to feel that it's our *Drum*, a real African *Drum*. . . . We like to see black faces, you know."

"You'll find it a job to get Coloureds to read an African paper," said Henry. "They don't like being associated with natives."

"Ag, they're getting better all the time, man," said Dan Twala. "When I was down in Cape Town for the soccer finals, those Coloureds gave me terrific times, man. They asked all the African boys to a ball, and no trouble; they've changed a lot, it's true."

"We don't want *Drum* to be racialist," said Andy, the Coloured printer.

"You'll never get Coloureds to read the *Drum*," said our agents. "They hate the natives more than the whites do."

We decided to try, cautiously, introducing Coloured features into *Drum*, while we watched closely the reactions of African and Coloured readers. We dropped the prefix "African" from *Drum*.

What were the tastes of Coloureds, and how did they differ from Africans? Andy was my guide into the Coloured community; and I soon found myself caught between not two worlds but three.

Andy, unlike most Coloureds, was not ashamed of his African blood. His father was a Scotsman, his mother a Basuto; and in his shrewd common sense, his gaiety and tolerance, he seemed to combine the best of both races. He was brought up in Basutoland, and felt the agony of the colour bar in reverse. The race-proud Basutos would taunt him in class and on the football field with being a white boy, and left him out of their games and jokes.

From Basutoland he moved to the cosmopolitan world of Johannesburg. He did well in business, and bought a printing shop. His friends were mainly Coloureds and Indians, but he always welcomed visiting Basutos, speaking vigorous Sotho alternately with his rich English. When Coloureds talked about Coloured rights or native servants, Andy would laugh and say, "I'm just a Basuto."

With his European way of life, and his Basuto blood and loyalties, Andy was a rare bridge between black and white.

He introduced me to a high-class Coloured shebeen near his printing shop, called Ma Parker's. It was in a world quite apart from the Back o' the Moon. The clientèle were more sedate and conventional, including a headmaster, a lawyer and several businessmen, and the conversation was more rational and prosaic. The friendly atmosphere was close to an English pub. At Ma Parker's you could drink on account and pay at the end of the month, and the brandy was never watered down.

The Coloureds at Ma Parker's talked endlessly about race. Shut off from the whites, and despising the blacks, they had no real world of their own. With Coloureds there could be none of the glib talk of apartheid theory, of "developing along their own lines", and "preserving their own culture". The Coloureds had been knocking on the doors of the white world ever since the whites first conceived them. In the back room of Ma Parker's, where people were shut out from civilised lives by being a shade darker than their brothers, apartheid showed itself in all its cruelty. They joked and laughed about apartheid, and about being mistaken for white men, and being called bushmen, hotnots, coolies, with compulsory wounding laughter.

"Tony, I must tell you," said Jackie, a dark-skinned Coloured clerk. "There's a white girl who rings up our office on business nearly every day, and I usually speak to her; so we start getting friendly and introduce each other over the phone. 'You sound so nice,' she says one day, 'I'd love to see what you look like.' Then a few days later she says, 'I've got to fetch something from your office this afternoon, so I'll be able to meet you.' So that afternoon in comes a pretty little white girl, and says, 'Which is Jackie?' And somebody points to me, and says, 'That's him.' You should have seen her face when she saw that Jackie was a Kaffir boy. Did I laugh!" And everyone laughed.

"Of course we white men don't talk to you bushmen," laughed Dick, a light-skinned Coloured teacher, with a fine presence. "You know, I used to have a Dutchman friend, who thought I

159

was white; he used to ask me into pubs, and I kept my hat firmly on my head, so that no one could see my kinky hair. One day he asked me to his home. I didn't want to go, because I couldn't ask him back to my bushman home, but I couldn't say no. So I went along with him to his house. In the front room was an old Coloured woman. 'Oh,' I thought, 'that must be the cook-girl. . . .' Then he turns round to me and says, 'Dick, let me introduce you to my mother. . . .' Was I surprised! He was as much a bushman as I was."

One evening Andy was driving me from Ma Parker's, with two light-skinned Coloured friends, Norman and Victor, who were both half-drunk. As we passed a European bar, Victor shouted: "Andy! Stop! I want to buy Tony a drink." Andy drove on, but Victor pulled at his arm, and he had to stop. "We can be white men any day, can't we, Norman?" said Victor. "Come along, Tony, we're having a drink. . . ."

"I'm staying here," said Andy. "I'm only a Basuto."

I followed unwillingly. I could see Victor's nervousness beneath his bravado. He walked in with Norman, talking loudly, ordered three brandies, and cracked a joke with the barman.

"Well, Tony, your health!" he said, winking, while I winced. Victor went on talking, introducing himself to the people around. At last he gulped down his drink. "Well, chaps, I'll be seeing you." He went back to the car, where Andy was waiting patiently.

"We can be Europeans, you see," said Victor, laughing with relief.

*   *   *

"Come out and meet Charles," said Andy one night. "He's a class writer. We'll try to get him to write stories for *Drum*. He's quite bitter these days. He used to be a headmaster, but he got into politics, and they fired him, poor chap. Life's tough for him now. But, hell, he can write. He won a prize for a story in a white paper once, but they wouldn't give it to him because he was a bushman."

We arrived to find Charles drunk. He was a huge hulk of a man, with rugged features, sprawled across the table in the small bare drawing-room.

Andy and I started talking about *Drum*, and the stories we wanted him to write. Charles looked me up and down with his piercing dark eyes, and muttered roughly in reply:

"Ag, you're messing about with words, man." He paused.

"You white men, you come to see us, but you're not our friends. We Coloured people—we didn't ask you to sleep with our black mothers. We didn't ask you to make bastards of us. And then you run away when our black mothers have children. You're our own cousins, man. And you don't even let us into your bioscopes. You cowards! You come and make friends with us, and then take our girls—and we can't take yours. . . ."

His friend, next to him, turned anxiously to me.

"You mustn't mind what he says; he doesn't mean it; he likes you, really. He's had a bit to drink, that's all."

Charles went on:

"Do you know what we'll do with you white people when the day comes? We'll kill you! You can't imagine with what relish I'll cut your throat. The African people are on the march—I'm telling you. I'm telling you. . . ."

"Please, Charles, please. Remember he's your guest. I'm so sorry, Mr. Sampson—he really doesn't mean it. . . ."

"I mean it! I mean it! We'll kill all the white men!"

"No, we don't want to kill them, Charles. We don't want a Mau Mau here, do we?" said the friend.

"Yes, we'll kill them. And then what? Then we'll marry their women. That's what we'll do."

His mountainous figure lunged across the table. His rough-hewn face, lit by the candle, stood out dimly from the darkness.

161

I caught Andy's eye and said it was time to be going. Charles looked up at me and said quietly:

"You'll come and see me again, won't you?"

*　　　*　　　*

One day at Ma Parker's when I was sitting with Andy and the regulars, I noticed a white man whom I had not seen before. He was silent and looked nervous, with a habit of chewing matches, and I felt that he had a grudge against me, the other white man in the company. When he left soon afterwards, I turned to Andy and said:

"Who was that white man?"

"Harry's not white," said Andy, "though he used to be. Now he's Coloured."

Andy told me his story. Harry was born in the Coloured community of a country town; he was brought up as Coloured, but he was very light-skinned, and people often mistook him for a European. When the war came, he decided to join the South African Air Force—as a white man. He would be away from his friends and neighbours, and there was nothing to show that he was Coloured. As a white man he could do more and earn more, and he was only one of the hundreds who "crossed the line" during the war. He did well, gained a commission, and made many white friends.

Then he was transferred to a unit where there was a white man from his home town. He recognised Harry—as a Coloured. He reported Harry to the authorities. He was cashiered and made to join the Cape Corps, the Coloured regiment.

After the war, Harry went back to his life as a Coloured and became a doctor. He made friends with Africans and Coloureds, and avoided the company of white men. Soon after I met him at Ma Parker's he left for England, and the argument over his colour was forgotten.

Harry was only one of thousands of "playwhites", as they

call the light-skinned Coloureds who "pass for white" and break away from the Coloured world. At Ma Parker's they were always telling stories about playwhites and their tricks. How they powder their faces to lighten them, use irons to straighten their hair, avoid sunshine, always wear a hat to hide their hair. How they're called Vensterkies, or "window-men", because when they see their old Coloured friends they stare into a shop window.

"But we can always recognise our own people," said Dick; "you'd be surprised how many so-called whites are Coloured. Everyone knows that—and—[naming two well-known white politicians] are Coloured. The other day I had to go and see a city councillor in a deputation; you know, as soon as I saw him, I could tell he wasn't only a bastard, but a Coloured bastard; and I knew that he knew that I knew."

"All my brothers are white, you know," said Norman. "I'm the only bushman in the family. Of course they get me liquor and things, but I can't earn the same money. And I can never go to the bioscope with them."

Nothing showed up the agony of apartheid more forcefully than the antics of men who had to disown their family to gain their freedom. It was common to have one half of a Coloured family playing white, while the other remained Coloured. There was often a wide range of colour within the family: the dread of every playwhite mother was to have a dark-skinned throwback child; there were stories of dark Coloured babies being left as orphans, rather than betray their mother's race.

Once I went to Dick's home, and he appeared carrying a pure white two-year-old child, with straight fair hair.

"Gentlemen, let me introduce you to the Herrenvolk," he said. "My son."

A tall blond white man came into the *Drum* office one morning.

"I want to write a story for *Drum*."

"We don't usually accept stories from Europeans."

"I'm not white, I'm Coloured: that's my story."

Charlie Cain, as he was called, told his story to Arthur, and we published it in the next month's *Drum*. "I was a white man."

He was born as a Coloured with Coloured parents; but Charlie had blond hair and blue eyes, with nothing to show he was not white. When he went to the Coloured school, he was singled out for teasing. "Wit boer!" they called him. "Why don't you go to a white school, eh?" Everywhere he was given a questioning look from his fellow Coloureds.

When he left school, a white woman who had befriended him suggested that he should find work as a white man. "After all I had gone through, in looks, sneers and dirty names, I decided to take her advice," he said. When he was sixteen, he found a job as an apprentice bricklayer on a mine; no one asked questions, or doubted that he was white. He had no difficulty in copying European manners or way of speech.

He still lived at Crown Mines Coloured location with his parents. He led a double life. At home he was Coloured, at work he was white. But he was in constant fear that his two worlds would meet. Travelling home by train one night, he met two white friends from the mine. "We'll walk home with you," they said to Charlie. "It's dangerous with the *tsotsis* around." "Don't bother," he said anxiously, "I'll be quite safe." But they insisted; terrified of his secret, he led them, not to the Coloured location, but to the European district adjoining it.

"This is my home," he said, stopping outside a dark house; "but I'm afraid I can't ask you in, because my people are asleep." They stood talking outside. "We must go home," they said at last. As they were leaving, Charlie started walking into the yard. The dogs barked. Charlie watched his friends turn round the corner, and fled back to the Coloured location.

Charlie worked well, and was soon earning seventeen pounds a week—far more than he could ever earn as a Coloured. But he found his two lives a perpetual strain. He met Brother

Olson, the missionary who had converted Gray, and joined his hymn-singing meetings. The deceptions of his situation became unbearable. "I'm going to give up being a white man," he told a Coloured friend. "And seventeen pounds a week? You're crazy, man!"

A few days later, his boss gave him a lift in his car. Charlie plucked up courage to tell him.

"Well, I won't say anything; you can stay on as you are; it makes no difference to me, provided you don't tell the others."

But Charlie would not continue the pretence. He left the job, and soon afterwards, as a Coloured, became a despatch clerk in a mail-order house, at four pounds a week. "Somehow that four pounds seemed more blessed," he said.

No one knows how many Coloureds have disappeared into the white world. One investigator, asking "How white is white South Africa?" estimated that over half a million whites have Coloured blood.[1] But no accurate method of calculation has been devised, either in South Africa or in America, where negroes similarly "pass for white."[2]

To the Nationalist government, this merging of the races was a nightmare: they were determined to establish the purity of the white race beyond doubt, and to find out who was, and who was not, white, Coloured and native. They have embarked on a great scheme of classification, and subjected people to every kind of humiliation to discover their race. Officials passed combs through the hair of Coloured men, and felt the lobes of their ears, in an attempt to prove that they were natives. In one case a man was classified as native, his brother as Coloured.

---

[1] Advocate George Findlay: *Miscegenation*. He bases his calculations on the 1921 census.

[2] For a thorough discussion of "playing white" and its implications, see Sheila Patterson, *Colour and Culture in South Africa*, pp. 182–185. For the American equivalent, see Gunnar Myrdel, *An American Dilemma*, pp. 129–130, 683–688.

Hundreds of whites were demoted to Coloureds, and Coloureds to natives; children with a trace of Coloured blood were expelled from white schools. But however arbitrary and ruthless the investigations have been, they have always stopped short of completeness: for, as every Coloured in South Africa knows, a too close investigation of the whiteness of the whites would produce results that would shake the theory of apartheid to its foundations.

At Ma Parker's the conversation always came back to race in the end. Blood, colour, skin. Kaffirs, Hotnots, coolies. Hats and hair. Half-moons on fingernails. Touch of the tar-brush. "He could play white any day." "I *thought* he'd changed his name." "So he's going out with a Coloured girl?" "Turk, my foot! He's just a bushman." "Anyone can *say* they're Portuguese."

The more we saw of the Coloured world, the more we realised the difficulties facing an inter-racial *Drum*. Could we ever escape from race? In the "pigmentocracy" of South Africa, skin colour was firmly linked with money and success. The slogan of apartheid echoed down the corridor of colour. Whites scorned playwhites, playwhites scorned Coloureds, Coloureds scorned natives, light Coloureds scorned dark Coloureds. I once saw a well-educated dark Coloured thrown out of a light Coloured party because of his skin.

The disease spread to Africans. Light-skinned Xhosas often succeeded in "playing Coloured", for the sake of extra privileges, better jobs and houses, and exemption from passes. They adopted a European name, cultivated Coloured friends and a Coloured accent, and talked disparagingly about "natives". We joked about one of these new Coloureds in our gossip column, and he sued us for libel. It raised an interesting point for our attorneys. Was it actually libellous to call someone an African? The case was withdrawn.

The more we tried to make *Drum* inter-racial the more firmly we came up against race. As soon as we introduced pictures of Coloureds, we had trouble with playwhites. A pretty light-skinned Coloured girl posed willingly for a fashion picture, but a day after it was published a hysterical mother rang us up. "Please take that picture out, sir. Nina's uncle says that if that photo appears in a native magazine, he'll have nothing to do with her. . . ." Some time later, Nina was seen walking with a white man. The crossing-over to the white camp of some of our best subjects was a constant annoyance. "What's happened to that girl who was lined up for a cover?" I asked Arthur. "Oh, she's white now. She won't come near us."

We persevered with an inter-racial *Drum*. In some ways, the Government was on our side: it was slowly uniting all other races against them. Coloureds who before aspired to become white, or looked forward to more rights, now found the doors slammed on them: they were forced to look towards the Africans as allies.

"The future lies on the Reef, with the Africans," a well-known Cape Town Coloured politician said to me. "We ought to join with them. . . ."

"Then why don't you?" I asked.

"Frankly, because I don't *like* them."

But after the defiance campaign, and the Government's new apartheid laws, there was a slow though reluctant trend towards Coloured–African co-operation.

Slowly our circulation in Coloured districts and in Cape Town, the Coloured stronghold, went up, and letters began to come from Coloured readers.

"It gives me great joy," wrote Vera Miya, "to see Africans, Indians, Coloureds and Europeans buying and reading *Drum*. I feel proud to observe this because it shows we are all climbing up the ladder of inter-racial understanding. . . ."

CHAPTER SIXTEEN

Taboo

Nothing aroused the hostility of white South Africa towards black more than the mention of mixed marriages and miscegenation. Nationalists, United Party and liberals were united in their dread of miscegenation and a "coffee-coloured nation." The Seretse Khama affair reverberated as a warning: the nationalists used pictures of Peggy Cripps with her African husband, Joseph Appiah, as election propaganda against the United Party. "Would you like *your* daughter to marry a black man?" A shiver went down the voter's spine.

This taboo made *Drum*'s job difficult. When we received photographs of American negroes with white wives, we had to cut out the wives. Mixed marriages were a favourite subject of the American negro magazines: *Ebony, Jet, Tan, Our World*. "My White Wife." "She Loved my Race." "I married a negro," were recurring themes, and covers often showed mixed couples. The magazines were banned in South Africa, with a penalty for possessing one of a thousand pounds.

The Immorality Act of 1927 (amended in 1950 to include Coloureds), and the Mixed Marriages Act of 1949, forbade relations between Europeans and non-Europeans, with a maximum penalty, nearly always applied, of six months' hard labour, without the option of a fine. Although numbers of convictions were made, they were little heard of.

"Ever been to Butch's?" said Jackie, a young Coloured, one night at Ma Parker's.

"No."

"And you think you know about Jo'burg! You haven't seen

life if you haven't been to Butch's. You'll get some stories there that'll make your *Drum* stand on end!"

Jackie took me to Butch's. I was becoming used to the odd destinations of my job.

We parked the car down a side street, near the middle of town, next to a large factory. As we stepped out, Jackie looked carefully round; there was no one in sight except an old Zulu sitting on a soap box listening to a friend and muttering long "aaaaahs."

"This way," said Jackie, and led the way down a narrow passage between two tall factory blocks into a small dark courtyard. The house in front of us had high gables, and looked like an early well-to-do Johannesburg dwelling house, in what used to be the fashionable quarter of town.

Jackie knocked on the door, three times, with a pause after the second knock. He looked up at a small window beside the door, and a moment later a black girl's face appeared at the window, looked down at Jackie and disappeared. A key turned in the lock, a latch was pulled and the door opened.

The girl closed the door behind us; she was petite and delicate, made up with bright-red lipstick and fingernails. She looked up at us haughtily.

"Hi, Yvonne," said Jackie; "Butch in?"

"Ya," said Yvonne grumpily.

Jackie beckoned me into a wide dark passage. He stood outside an open door, and said:

"Butch."

"Who's it?" came a gruff voice.

"Charlie," said Jackie, and pushed the door open.

It was a large, heavily furnished room. A dim light came from a bare bulb hanging from the ceiling. Murky landscapes hung from the dark yellowy walls.

A white man sat in an armchair by a smouldering fire, with his feet up. He wore a shabby hat on the back of his head. He looked round without moving his head.

169

"Huh, Jackie. Siddown." He waved an arm.

"Butch, this is Johnny. Journalist."

"Last journalist came here I kicked out of that window. Won't come here again. Taught him. Kicked him out."

I sat down with Jackie. Butch said roughly:

"Yvonne. Half straight. Three glasses."

Yvonne swayed out, kicking her bare feet up behind her. A short pink-faced bearded man with sharp blue eyes walked in. He jerked his head around nervously, his eyes darting all over the room.

"Hallo, Oscar," said Jackie.

"Hiya! Hiya!" said Oscar, nodding vigorously, and grinning through his black beard. He turned to me, nodded again, and said, "Hiya! Hiya!" and went to sit down on the couch by the window. He sat eagerly forward, with his pink hands rubbing his knees, as if something was about to happen.

"Beauty been in yet, Butch?" said Oscar, fidgeting with his hands.

"Bitch's upstairs," said Butch.

"How's Yvonne, Butch? Eh, Butch? Eh?"

"Bitch," said Butch.

"Ye-es! Big bitch," said Oscar.

"I told her where to get off, I showed her," said Butch.

"Ye-es, it's true!" Oscar bounced. "He slapped her right on the cheek, man. That showed her, didn't it, Butch?"

"Huh. She's a deep bitch, that one. But I showed her," said Butch.

Just then Oscar's round eyes lit up, and he bounced on the sofa. I looked round, and a tall black girl in a long taffeta dress walked in, with her large sad eyes downcast and her mouth just open in a look either of mystery or vacancy. She looked up as Oscar caught her eye, patted the sofa beside him and nodded hard. She sat down carefully, at the opposite end of the sofa to Oscar, and Oscar nodded, and plucked at his beard twice, and manoeuvred with his feet so that he moved slightly up the sofa.

"Hi, Beaut! Hi!" said Oscar, beaming out of his beard, and still jerking his head in excitement.

"Good evening, Mr. Oscar," said the girl slowly, pronouncing "evening" with three syllables.

I watched the two together—the pink, tense little man, and the slow brown girl, moving her brown eyes up and down, while his blue eyes jumped round her body. He talked in quick, staccato sentences, while she murmured, "Yes, Mister Oscar. No, Mister Oscar," in long syllables.

"Where shall we go, Beaut? Nice little car, Beaut! Quite safe! Barberton? Eh? Piet Retief? Durban? Nice sand dunes in Durban! Nice joints! Cape Town eh, Beaut? It's safe there, eh?"

"Six months, Mister Oscar, without the option of a fine," said Beaut.

I heard three knocks on the outside door.

Yvonne came mincing in. "Bitch-never-die."

"Huh. Okay," said Butch.

A big black woman appeared. Her hard face was overlaid in paint and powder, and her huge mouth drooped from a swollen upper lip. She looked between forty and fifty. Her tight green dress showed the sharp curves of her figure. She looked tired, except for her warm restless eyes.

"Hiya, Mr. Butch," she said in a cracked voice.

"Just out?" said Butch.

"Three days, Mr. Butch."

"Back at work?"

"Ya. Business bad. Tough, Mr. Butch."

Yvonne poured out brandy for Butch, Jackie and me.

"Her too," said Butch, jerking his head at Bitch-never-die.

Oscar patted the empty end of his sofa. Bitch-never-die looked quickly at Butch, and walked over to Oscar.

"Maud still inside?" said Butch.

"Ya. Third time, man! It's tough for Maud," said Bitch-never-die.

"Hester?"

"She's out, Mr. Butch. Back at work."

"Phyllis?"

"They caught her, man! With a white guy in a Plymouth. Poor Phylly."

"Stupid bitch," said Butch. "I knew she'd get caught. I told her."

"It's true," said Oscar, looking at me. "Butch told her, didn't you, Butch?"

Again three knocks. Yvonne appeared.

"Queenie."

"Okay." Butch turned to Jackie. "Huh—Queenie: the Queen of the Streets!"

"It's true," said Oscar.

Queenie came in. She was white. She was big, handsome in her way, with an open, rosy face and wild hair; she swayed her large hips as she walked in, and looked round the room imperiously. Her eyes were still young, but her mouth was set hard, with lines down her jowl.

"Good evening, Mr. Butch, eh?" said Queenie, in an Afrikaans accent. She looked round and saw Bitch-never-die.

"Hi—Bitchie! How's it, dearie?" And she cackled dryly: "Business bad, isn't it?"

"We's too many, my dear," said Bitch-never-die, laughing with her whole body. "But that white guy shifted fast when he saw the cop."

"Same beat with Queenie?" said Butch, lifting his eyebrows at Bitch-never-die.

"Yes, Mr. Butch!" she grinned with zig-zag teeth.

"Up-down, up-down—cross in the middle!" said Queenie, shaking her hands in opposite directions. "Blankes one side, Nie-Blankes the other!"

Another young white man walked in, wearing a brown lumber-jacket. He muttered quietly: "Butch. Oscar. Jackie. Bitchie. Queenie. Beaut. Mister." He nodded at each of us.

"Jose been back yet?" he said quietly to Butch.

"Nah. That bitch won't be back for a week, man. *How* much did you give her?"

"Fifteen. She wanted a dress."

"Huh. A week. You ask that one"—he nodded towards the kitchen—"she knows. They're deep, these bitches. I told you."

"It's true!" said Oscar. "You know, Van, Butch told you! Didn't you, Butch?"

Butch pushed round his chair, tipped his hat farther back, and stared at me.

"You know what? You're a journalist, aren't you? You know what goes on in Jo'burg, don't you? Well, I'm telling you, you know nothing. I'm the guy knows. These bitches tell me. Everything."

"It's true," said Oscar. "Butch knows."

"You think it's apartheid in Jo'burg, don't you? You think it's blacks in Orlander, and whites in Houghton. Don't you?"

"Yes," I said.

"Well, you're wrong. No such thing. You ask these bitches. Ask them about white men—like Oscar and Van, there."

"It's true," said Oscar.

"You know what?" he said, pausing to look me up and down, "I know enough about some of these big white bosses you see in Jo'burg in their Cadillacs to break them. They know Butch. You ask these bitches. Eh, Beaut?"

"It's true, Mr. Butch," said Beauty sadly.

"You know nothing, you journalists. You think black men don't dance with white girls in Jo'burg, don't you? You know nothing, man. You ask the managing director of—Stores about Butch. I could take you to places which make you gasp, man— right in the middle of your white Jo'burg. Right under your

173

blerry noses. You know what? I was a cop. I know things. I know what cops do. Huh. Apartheid. You think there's no white men in Orlander and Moroker. You know what? Black likes white and white likes black."

"It's true," said Oscar, grinning from the couch. "Eh, Beaut?" Beauty gazed up.

I caught Jackie's eye, and Jackie nodded and got up. "See you some more, Butch," said Jackie.

"Huh," said Butch, and closed his eyes.

"Hiya! Hiya!" said Oscar, nestling against Bitch-never-die. "See you some more, eh?"

Yvonne let us out, glowered, and banged the door.

"See what I mean," said Jackie, as I looked round the quiet courtyard. "That's the real Jo'burg. That's the heart of Africa."

*　　　*　　　*

I could not agree; but I found, from the stories that reached *Drum*, that there was some truth in what Butch had said. In spite of, or because of, the strict apartheid and severe penalties, the races were still drawn towards each other. Once Jackie pointed out to me a white man picking up a black girl at a street corner.

"I'm the result," he said. "A million Coloureds isn't bad going. . . . Why do you think the whites hate the blacks so much? Have you listened to a middle-aged spinster shouting at a young African boy? Have you ever watched an Afrikaner cop handling an African girl? What's that if it isn't sex?"

It is one of the absurd by-products of apartheid, that each side builds up a legend about the other. Blacks think that whites have exceptional virility, and vice-versa. The stories that white men circulate about black girls are the same as the stories that black men tell about white girls. The forbidden fruit is the more tempting.

*　　　*　　　*

One afternoon a young German doctor called Kurt walked into the *Drum* office, hand-in-hand with a Coloured girl, and asked for a photograph of an African beauty. The Coloured girl clung to his side, and they walked out together with the photograph.

"He's going to get into trouble," said Henry.

Two months later we were sorting readers' votes for *Drum*'s "Miss Africa" beauty contest. The winner was a sultry beauty called Maisie. Henry knew her and went out to Orlando to present her with fifty pounds. He was told that Maisie had just gone to jail: she had been caught with a white man. We quickly selected the next winner, less beautiful but more respectable.

Three months later, Kurt came into the office again; his head was shaved close, and his face thin. He said he had just been to jail for four months. He was the man who had been caught with our Miss Africa. "Maisie's due out tomorrow," he said. "I'm going to meet her at the jail."

The Immorality Act was designed to keep the white race pure and separate: but sometimes it was difficult to say exactly who *was* white. Often in court there was argument over a man's race. Once in Cape Town a white man living with a Coloured girl, with three children by her, was charged under the "Im Act". He pleaded, in defence, that he was not white, although he had voted and bought liquor as a white man—but Coloured. The magistrate acquitted the couple.

"However," he added, "if he *wants* to be a Coloured man, he must be branded once and for all as such." At the second hearing, he apologised for using the word "branded".[1]

One Saturday morning, at our monthly *Drum* conference, Henry said:

"I've got a story. Next door to me in Orlando, there's a white woman living with a black police sergeant. . . ." No one believed it.

[1] For this and similar cases, see *Colour and Culture in South Africa* by Sheila Patterson, pp. 141–143.

"She can't really be white!" "Isn't she an albino?" "Must be playing white. . . ."

Henry insisted that she was a pure white girl, living happily and openly with her African husband.

We decided not to pursue the story: anything we said would either be libellous, or lead to a conviction. I forgot about the White Woman of Orlando.

Four months later, a white woman, Regina Brooks, and an African police sergeant, Richard Kumalo, were arrested in Orlando and charged under the Immorality Act.

When Regina Brooks appeared in court, she was described as "a European housewife, living in Orlando". But apart from her features, everything about her was African. She wore a simple cloth, or *doek*, tied over her hair, like an African girl. She had a two-year-old Coloured child strapped to her back, in the African fashion. She spoke Zulu, and claimed to speak no English. She had the relaxed, unquestioning look of a simple African woman. She seemed quite unashamed by the charge and the publicity she was facing. She was plain and without make-up; but there was a suggestion of beauty in her face, and a dignity in her bearing.

Richard Kumalo was a well-built rugged Zulu, with holes in the lobes of his ears for the traditional Zulu plugs. He spoke English with difficulty.

Charged with co-habiting with an African, Regina's defence was that she was herself an African. Although her features were European, she said she had "gone native". She lived as an African, and was accepted as one. She had no white friends.

The case aroused extraordinary interest. Here was a white woman admitting quite proudly that she had gone native—the most dreaded fate of any white South African. To the Europeans it was a betrayal. To Africans, on the other hand, "Linda Malinga", as she called herself, became a heroine: a white woman, proud to live among Africans and call herself black.

The courtroom was jammed with African spectators; outside, a crowd of two thousand thronged round her car to catch sight of her.

Henry persuaded Regina to tell him, in Zulu, her life story for *Drum*.

Regina was born at a small farm in the Orange Free State, the tenth of eleven children; her father was English, and died before she was two. In the colour-blind time of childhood, she spent more time with the black servants on the farm than with her white brothers and sisters. She learnt to speak Sesuto and Zulu more fluently than English. She often ate with the servants in the kitchen, and stayed in their homes.

She went to a white school, but was unhappy: she couldn't understand her schoolmates, or play with them. Then she went to stay with her sister Anna, who had married an Afrikaans farmer called Viljoen.

Anna, too, was happier among Africans than among whites. Soon after she married Viljoen, she fell in love with an African, Alpheus Mlilo, and had a child by him; she was charged and fined fifty pounds, which Viljoen paid for her. Mlilo was banished from the district for three years; but as soon as he returned he went to see Anna again; and some time after she gave birth to a Coloured girl. This time both Mlilo and Anna were sentenced to six months in prison. Viljoen divorced Anna and gave her one thousand pounds.

Regina went back to live on the farm with her mother. This time she went to an African school, and was happy. In the next years she had two African boyfriends; everyone called her "Linda Malinga".

One day she went to an African wedding at a nearby farm, with the usual dancing, drinking and feasting. There she met Richard Kumalo, who had come up from Johannesburg. They fell in love. Some time later, Kumalo asked her to come up and join him in a new house he had just rented in Orlando. The people in Orlando were surprised to find a white woman among them, dressed like an African, speaking Zulu, and carrying a baby on her back. At first they kept away from her, but in time they accepted her proudly as one of them.

But Kumalo already had an African wife. He saw nothing wrong by tribal custom with having two wives, in different houses. But his first wife thought otherwise; when she found out about the new white woman, she told the police. One evening the police called at the house in Orlando, and found Kumalo and Regina together. They were arrested and charged. . . .

"I don't like white people," Regina told Henry. "I couldn't be happy among them; I've never felt at ease with the way they behave. I can't imagine myself being employed as a white woman, because I can't behave as a white woman. Besides, what would happen to my Coloured daughter, Tandi? Everyone ends up calling me Linda Malinga."

Regina's life story was her defence: she had lived as an African, and was accepted by Africans. But the magistrate held that she was still a European, and sentenced her to six months; she appealed, and was granted bail. When bail money was needed, a hat was passed round the huge crowd of Africans outside the court, and filled with money.

Six months later, in the Supreme Court, Regina won her appeal.

"I am of the opinion," said Mr. Justice de Wet, "that the Crown has not established that Regina Brooks is a European within the meaning of the act."

"I will call friends and slaughter an ox and there will be great feasting at our home," said Kumalo when he heard the news. But Regina had vanished. A few days later she was found with an African friend.

"I have left Mr. Kumalo," she said; "we were not meant for each other."

CHAPTER SEVENTEEN

We Won't Move

Of all the African townships on the Reef, the most lively, important and sophisticated was Sophiatown. It was Limehouse, Chelsea, Tottenham Court Road and Surbiton rolled into one. Dr. Alfred Xuma, Jazzboy, Job Rathebe, Dolly Rathebe, Horror and Can Themba all lived in Sophiatown. The House of Truth, Father Huddleston's mission, Back o' the Moon and the headquarters of the "Americans" were all in Sophiatown. In its crowded and narrow streets walked philosophers and gangsters, musicians and pickpockets, short-story writers and businessmen. Sophiatown embodied all that was best and worst of African life in towns.

Sophiatown was unique because, alone of the African townships, it was part of Johannesburg. Its steep tarred streets led down to the outskirts of the city, four miles from the centre. There was no fence round Sophiatown, as there is at Western Native Township or Pimville, and no policemen to examine permits at the gate. Houses could be bought or sold by Africans, with freehold rights. There was no superintendent to allocate houses, as at Orlando or Jabavu. Sophiatown was a free township, free to go to hell its own way.

I used to drive to Sophiatown through the prim white suburb of Westdene, where the neat detached bungalows each had their garage, garden and stoep; the streets were quiet and empty, except for an occasional American car taking the family to the bioscope, or a native servant returning home.

At the edge of Westdene, the road ended abruptly, facing

179

a narrow strip of rough ground. Opposite was Sophiatown. The two townships, white Westdene and black Sophiatown, glowered at each other across no-man's-land.

Across the strip of land was a different universe. The streets were filled with Africans, talking, singing and shouting until late at night. The decaying houses, with shacks spawned all round them, were overflowing with people. Jazz beat from the crowded rooms.

Sophiatown, the oldest of the African townships, was first established in 1905, next to a sewage farm in the bare veld, where no Europeans were likely to want to live. Johannesburg was then a young mining town, with an uncertain future. But as more gold was discovered, so Johannesburg spread out like an avalanche, surrounding Sophiatown with European townships. Europeans resented the "black spot" in their midst.

"When I first came to live in Toby Street, which is the boundary of Sophiatown, twenty-five years ago," said Dr. Xuma, "I faced open veld and spent quiet Sunday afternoons under the streets where Westdene now is. Today, across a narrow field, I face an array of European houses. . . . Why should Europeans, who object to our proximity, settle in the neighbourhood of Africans, when the whole of Johannesburg is theirs to choose from?"

As long ago as 1937, the United Party, with an eye on the marginal constituency of Westdene, began to cry, "Remove the Black Spots." But the expense and complications of moving sixty thousand people were formidable, and after the elections, the black spots were forgotten.

When Malan was voted into power in 1948, Sophiatown presented a challenge to apartheid: the old issue was taken up with renewed fervour. In 1953 the "Western Areas Resettlement Act" was put before Parliament, proposing to remove Sophiatown.

The plan was to build a new location for the residents of

Sophiatown with the inviting name of Meadowlands, nine miles out of Johannesburg, adjoining the big African locations of Orlando, Moroka, Jabavu and Pimville. Like them, Meadowlands would have little brick box-houses of three rooms, owned and controlled by the municipality, who would rent them to tenants. No freehold ownership would be allowed.

The government claimed that the proposed removal was a slum clearance scheme, and pointed to the broken-down shacks and leaking houses of Sophiatown.

"The Western Areas removal scheme is not only in the interests of the European community of Johannesburg, it is also in the interests of the natives who live there," said Dr. Verwoerd in the Senate. "The chances that natives will have a healthier and happier life are far greater in this new area. . . ."

It was true that Sophiatown contained hideous slums; but the hessian tents of Moroka and the breeze-block Shelters of Orlando were far worse, and there was no reason why Sophiatown houses should not be rebuilt on the same site. The real motive for the scheme was apartheid. Africans would be removed from a European area and by being deprived of freehold rights they could have no permanent claim to live in urban areas.

The scheme aroused immediate opposition from European liberals, bishops, rabbis and even the United Party. The Sophiatown move was the most extensive apartheid operation yet planned.

Father Huddleston organised a Western Areas protest committee. Dr. Xuma formed a sedate "Western Areas anti-expropriation and proper housing committee". "A Meadowlands house would fit quite easily into this room," he said, waving round his Sophiatown drawing-room.

The African National Congress stirred themselves for the first time since the defiance campaign two years before. They called for five thousand volunteers to organise opposition to the move.

The African and Indian Congresses held a joint protest meeting.

"The attempted uprooting of the people, and the destruction of the right to own land, are the most flagrant violations of human rights and elementary decency," said a resolution. Police with rifles invaded the hall and took the names of everyone present.

But the act was passed, and late in 1954 the first small brick houses began to rise in Meadowlands. Homeless Africans nearby threatened to squat in the houses, and police stood guard over the empty shells.

One morning in January, 1955, one hundred and fifty-two families in Sophiatown received notices:

> You are hereby required in terms of the Native Resettlement Act 1954 to vacate the premises in which you reside by February 12, 1955.

As February 12 approached, the tension in Sophiatown rose. The government warned Europeans to keep away from the township. Police reinforcements were drafted to the area. Overseas journalists gathered expectantly in Johannesburg.

A few days before the move, I drove round Sophiatown. Police flying-squad cars moved slowly along the crowded streets, followed by jeers. Slogans were scrawled on the walls: WE WON'T MOVE. . . . THIS IS HOME. . . . HANDS OFF SOPHIATOWN. . . . *Tsotsis*, walking in gangs, chanted a new song in *tsotsi* Afrikaans—"Ons Daak Nie" ("We ain't quittin'.") Girls had Congress skirts and caps, and men carried Congress umbrellas, and wore the Congress uniform of plain khaki cloth. "It's untouched by white hands."

At the House of Truth, Can, P-boy and David were examining pamphlets picked up in Sophiatown. "ONS DAAK NIE," said one, printed by Congress in *tsotsi* Afrikaans. "That white fool Huddleston and his Communists are your enemies," said another, mysteriously dropped from a car. "Be ready to obey the call of the African National Congress," said another. "The government have declared war on the African people. . . . Africans in the Western Areas are in the front line of defence."

What would Congress do? Sophiatown was full of rumours. Would they resist, faced with five years' imprisonment? "Resha's got a secret 'M plan' for the twelfth," said somebody. "The code word is 'dancing the squares'."

"It was the best of times, the worst of times," I quoted to Can. "Is that right?"

"Funny, the *Tale of Two Cities* is a big hit in Sof'town. . . . But it isn't the best of times for us. We like security."

We visited P-boy at the "House of Commons", a small room in a dark backyard. The room was empty, but on the table was an open book—*A Tale of Two Cities*. "What did I tell you?" said Can.

We went to the Back o' the Moon.

"Hiya, Mr. Tony. Why haven't you been to my Nice Times?" said Fatsy. We sat and listened. "I'm telling you, sis," said Fatsy to another woman, "I ain't goin' to these Meadowlands! Back o' the Moon is staying right here! You can tell that to Dr. Verwoerd!" And she shook with giggling.

"It'll need a bulldozer to move me, brother, I'm telling you," said a lorry-driver on the couch; "do you know the price of beers in Orlando? Six shillings, if you're lucky."

"My father says that when the police come to move him, he's going to sit on our stoep with a gun," said a schoolboy. "It'll be over his dead body."

We went up to Dad, sitting by the fireplace.

"What's going to happen on the twelfth?" asked Can.

"We are united in our struggle against the forces of tyranny, sir," said Dad, staring at me.

"But what's going to happen on the twelfth, Dad?"

"We had our plans. We will obey the call—just you wait."

A week before the move, Father Huddleston opened an exhibition of photographs of Sophiatown in protest against the removal. Patrick Duncan came up from Basutoland to speak.

"I am prepared to stand shoulder to shoulder with anyone in Sophiatown who will resist."

"By saying that," he said afterwards, "I could be sentenced to five years' imprisonment."

Four days before the twelfth, a proclamation was issued, banning gatherings of more than ten people throughout the Reef.

Police pasted up copies of the proclamation on the walls of Sophiatown. Two detectives called on Father Huddleston, with a copy of the proclamation. Reinforcements of police cars appeared in Sophiatown, nosing their way through the crowded streets, looking for gatherings of more than ten people.

At six o'clock the same evening, loudspeaker cars announced that the first families would be moved to Meadowland at six a.m. next morning, February 9.

I drove to Sophiatown at dawn. The strip of land facing Westdene was blocked by eighty armed lorries with flying-squad cars, vans, motor-cycles and armed police.

Two thousand police waited in Sophiatown. They stood at every corner, looking grimly at the people walking to work. They cordoned off the two streets scheduled for removal.

I had coffee with Can at the House of Truth, and we waited for six o'clock. At the next-door house, people were moving their belongings in an old cart to another part of Sophiatown, to avoid being moved to Meadowlands. Father Huddleston strode past in his cassock, with Robert Resha, the stocky Congress leader. A policeman stepped up to them, and reminded them of the ban on gatherings.

Dr. Alfred Xuma looked out of his window to see an army assembled in front of his house. Sophiatown took on the look of a war zone. Overseas journalists drove round the township, looking for signs of impending trouble.

Just after six o'clock, engines revved, motor-cycles roared, and one by one the lorries drove into Sophiatown with military precision, to the houses scheduled for evacuation. Furniture, stoves and bedding were lifted from the ramshackle huts into the lorries, while puzzled children watched.

Two hours later, the lorries drove in a convoy to Meadowlands, with the tenants sitting high above the stacked furniture. The six-mile route was lined with armed police, while the homely African families drove past on their high perches, some singing "To Meadowlands we will go. . . ."

As the lorries left, demolition squads climbed on to the roofs of the deserted hovels and battered them down with pick-axes and sledge-hammers. By the end of the day the houses once teeming with families were a pile of rubble. Sophiatown was disappearing.

No one resisted. Nothing happened. There was no demonstration. The families left peacefully for Meadowlands.

"We Won't Move" on the walls remained to taunt Congress. "What could we do, with two thousand police?" they said. "We want action," demanded the Youth League. "Do something."

Four days after the move, Can and Bob woke me up at my flat at two o'clock in the morning.

"We've just come from a meeting in Sophiatown," said Can. "They're trying to organise a strike. They say they're going to start hitting the telegraph poles at three o'clock, to wake everyone up. I remember the last time they hit the telegraph poles—it was before the 1950 riots."

Can went off to fetch Jurgen, while I drove to Sophiatown with Bob.

An unnatural stillness lay over the township. The last drunks had gone to bed, and the early workers were not yet up. The

185

streets were empty except for bands of *tsotsis*. One group danced in front of my car.

"Who are you, baasie?"

"I'm from *Drum*."

"Okay, Mr. Drum, go on!"

I saw Robert Resha, sitting in a car in a dark corner. Three flying-squad cars patrolled round, peering at me as they passed.

Soon after three, I heard the sharp shrill noise of a steel telegraph pole being hit by a bar, like a ghostly, high-pitched bell. It pierced the silent township. The noise was taken up from behind, and from the side, till all Sophiatown seemed to shriek with the thin cry.

We followed the noise. *Tsotsis* were running from pole to pole, knocking them with iron bars, and dancing and shouting. As we passed, one of them shouted "Laanis!" "I don't like the way he said that," said Can.

Was this the beginning of a riot, the *tsotsis'* revenge for the humiliation of the move, their answer to "Do something?" Were they Congress, or *tsotsis* pretending to be Congress, or somewhere between? Resha drove slowly round.

"Is anything going to happen?" I asked.

"I should stay around."

Half an hour later, Sophiatown was filled with flying-squad cars. They screeched round the corners pursuing the pole-hitters. They caught a group of *tsotsis* hitting a pole. Two policemen jumped from the moving car, and raced after the fleeing *tsotsis*. They came back heaving a bedraggled youth between them. I felt, as I had felt before, that I was watching a game I did not understand, of Afrikaner v. African, with Englishmen on the touchline.

The police cars multiplied. The clang of poles faded out. I parked my car in a dark corner, and watched the squad cars passing, and *tsotsis* peeping round the corners.

A police car drew up beside me, and a large man stepped out.

I recognised him as Major Spengler, the head of the Special (Political) branch of the C.I.D., a familiar figure at Congress meetings.

"Good morning, Mr. Sampson." I started at hearing my name. "And what are you expecting here?"

"I thought there might be trouble," I said.

"Oh, I don't think so. We've got ten police cars here, you know." We chatted.

"Well, I'll see you around."

A group of Congress men appeared, wearing armbands, and looking dignified and all-knowing. A police car turned the corner. The Congress men dispersed at a run. The police car drove past, and they regained their dignity. They stood threateningly by the bus stop, where the first workers were queuing. A police car drove up and parked by the bus stop. The Congress men hurried away.

By six o'clock, all was normal in Sophiatown. The buses left with workers to town, while police cars stood by. The strike had failed.

The C.I.D. car pulled up again beside me. Major Spengler called out:

"Well, Mr. Sampson, I suppose we can be going home now?"

"I think so, yes."

"I hear you're going back to England very soon?"

How did he know? I wondered.

"You must be glad to be leaving South Africa, aren't you?"

"I've grown quite fond of it."

"But I'm sure you'll be glad to get back to England. Good-bye!"

The Sophiatown move still continues. It will be three years before the township has finally disappeared.

The slogans on the walls remain: WE WON'T MOVE. . . .

But what could they do?

CHAPTER EIGHTEEN

Harmonie

Nearly three years after Mr. Drum's visit to Bethal, a case appeared in court concerning the killing of a farm labourer, which achieved much publicity. This time it was not at Bethal, but in the Northern Transvaal, near the quiet country town of Rustenburg, "the town of rest", eighty miles from Johannesburg.

The accused was a wealthy, religious and respected farmer called Johannes Snyman, who lived at a farm called Harmonie.

Snyman, with the help of his son Matthys, and his African foreman Jantjie, had flogged Elias Mpikwa, an African labourer at Harmonie, with a hosepipe. They went on flogging him till they were tired. He died, a deformed corpse, the same day.

The trial at Rustenburg, with a jury consisting mainly of local Afrikaner farmers, became a *cause célèbre*. The jury's mild verdict of "common assault" surprised everyone, including the judge. Johannes Snyman was sentenced to eighteen months' imprisonment, and his son to six months'. But the unpleasant details which came to light in the trial, and the fate of Elias Mpikwa, remained in the minds of liberal South Africans.

Not long after the Snyman trial, I had a message from a friend in Rustenburg. "Why doesn't Mr. Drum have a look round here?" he said. "Rustenburg's getting almost as bad as Bethal. . . ."

I drove out with Henry to Rustenburg to discuss it. Apart from the Snyman case, two other Africans had been killed by Europeans in the district in the previous year. Peter Breedt had punched and kicked an African to death in a Rustenburg street,[1] and the brothers Gouws were found guilty of assaulting Joseph Mokwatsi with a rubber hosepipe and pushing his head in with their feet until he died with a broken neck.[2] Snyman himself had been previously convicted of assaulting an African labourer.

"Part of the trouble," said my friend, "is the system of convict labour. The prisons hire out labour for ninepence a day, and the farmers can do what they like with them. Poor Mpikwa, you see, was a ninepence-a-day man. It's much cheaper than the ordinary four-pounds-a-month wage; and some farmers even get their own labourers charged and convicted so that they can get them back for ninepence a day."

"You can be sure that only a few of the cases come to light," he went on, "and according to my information, there's still a good deal of flogging going on round here. My grapevine tells me that Harmonie hasn't improved much since the court case. I think you should have a look round," he said, looking at Henry.

"Of course, I've had some farming experience at Bethal," Henry laughed. "Do you think they'd give me a job?"

"They must be quite short of labour, with the reputation they've got; but they'll be suspicious, you know. It's hardly natural, someone wanting a job at Harmonie."

A few days later, Henry set out gaily for Koster, the small village near Harmonie. He wore his oldest clothes, with two days' growth on his chin, and carried a few belongings tied up in a white sheet over his shoulder. We planned that he should spend two days in Koster, picking up the local gossip and looking round Harmonie, and then report back to the office.

Next day I received a telegram from Koster.

HAVE TAKEN JOB AT SNYMANS FARM STOP PLEASE SEND FOUR POUNDS HENRY.

[1] Johannesburg *Star*. 10/4/54.
[2] *Rand Daily Mail*. 22/5/54.

Five days later, Henry reappeared in the office, still cheerful, but visibly shaken.

"How did you get on?"

He turned up the bruised palms of his hands, and tapped his buttocks. "It was tough!" He went straight to his typewriter.

When Henry arrived in Koster, he found some friends, and heard the local news. Yes, they told him, things were pretty bad around Koster. Some farmers were still getting ninepence-a-day men from the prisons, in spite of their reputation. There was a farmer called "Jy Moet," (You Must) because he had a trick of holding down his workers and sjambokking them, shouting "Jy moet" as he did it.

Conditions hadn't improved much at Harmonie, they said, although the two Snymans were still in jail. Another white man was looking after the farm, who wasn't much better. Since the publicity from the case, Harmonie had been very short of labour. It might be possible to get a job there, but they didn't recommend it.

Henry walked off to Harmonie barefoot, with his white bag over his shoulder, like a "farm Kaffir". He knocked at the door of the farmhouse, and asked to see the baas. A hefty young white man in khaki shorts appeared, looking like a rugby player.

"Please, baas, I want work," said Henry in Kaffir Afrikaans.

The baas asked him some questions. Henry said he came from Magaliesburg, in the country.

"Got a pass?" said the baas, and Henry showed him his old George Magwaza pass, left over from his Bethal days. "All right; four pounds a month, with mealies. Next month you'll get five."

Henry was told to wait until the workers came back from the fields. They arrived, led by a tall tough-looking toothless "boss-boy" (as African foreman are called); he heard someone call him "Jantjie" and realised that he was the boss boy who had assisted in the killing of Elias Mpikwa. After a few questions from Jantjie, Henry joined in with the other labourers. They had their evening meal, of half-cooked porridge and skimmed milk, with half a cupful of brown sugar for eighteen men. One of the labourers, called "Slow Coach", showed Henry the compound, with a bare floor to sleep on, and a few sacks for bedclothes. He lay awake all night in his clothes, wondering if he could hear the ghost of Mpikwa who, said the labourers, still haunted the compound.

Henry worked from five in the morning till seven at night, weeding between the rows of maize that stretched far into the distance. He was watched and cursed by Jantjie for working too slowly as he stumbled along the hot fields, exhausted and miserable, with sore hands and an aching back.

During the brief meal-times, and in the evenings, he talked with his fellow-labourers. They told him gruesome stories about what had happened at the farm, and about Johannes Snyman, whom they called "Umabulal umuntu", or "he who killed a man." None of them had passes, they said, so that they could not leave the farm without being arrested. But they did not seem unhappy. They chatted cheerfully about their women, and told elaborate lies about what they had seen in Johannesburg, and the skyscrapers in the African locations. Henry acted the part of a simple country boy, and said nothing.

He had intended to stay at Harmonie for five days, but on the fourth day something changed his mind.

It had been a particularly gruelling day, in the fierce heat of the African high summer. It started raining, and when Henry went for shelter, Jantjie chased him back, and he worked on, soaked to the skin. When they stopped work at seven, Henry went up to Jantjie, and told him that the work was too hard for him, and he couldn't go on. Jantjie roared with laughter.

"On this farm you don't just quit when you want to. But it's not my farm—you'd better speak to the baas."

Henry went to see the baas, and told him the work was too

hard. He told Henry not to be lazy, called for Jantjie, and ordered him to chase Henry at work the next day. He sent Jantjie away, and asked Henry for his pass. He took it, and tore it slowly up into small pieces, and threw them on to the lawn.

"Now you haven't got a pass," he said, "you can't leave without my permission. I can have you arrested and put in jail. If you don't want to work fast like the others, I'll hand you over to the police and have you charged for refusing to work." Henry was about to walk off, when the baas beckoned him and led him to a bathroom in the outer house, and shut the door.

Henry waited, feeling sick. The white man repeated what he had said. "If Jantjie complains about your work, I'll beat you up and then have you arrested." Suddenly, he clapped Henry on the cheek with his open hand, and told him to lean over and face the wall. Henry bent down. Three hard kicks with a heavy boot.

"Now stand up." Henry faced the baas. "Now will you work hard tomorrow?"

"Yes, baas."

The white man struck him again on the cheek. "Hard work—rubbish! . . . Go away."

Henry ran back to the compound and told the others what had happened. They gasped at his impudence.

"You're lucky to get away so lightly. He-who-killed-a-man would have had you beaten up, and then put you in sacks so you couldn't run away." They laughed. "You wait, what's coming to you tomorrow!"

Henry said nothing; he decided to escape that evening.

When his room-mates were asleep, he tiptoed out of the compound, leaving some possessions behind. He passed through the Snyman gate with his heart thumping, and walked cautiously along the side of the main road, ducking behind a hedge whenever a car passed, fearful that the baas had already found him missing. At last he reached Koster, and took refuge for the night with his friends. Next morning, he was driven to the station. The police were there, inspecting passes.

"There's a labourer escaped from one of the farms," someone said. Henry waited in the car, and slipped on to the train just as it was leaving. He came back to Johannesburg, and safety, and wrote his story.

The calm, premeditated courage of Henry's visit was his greatest achievement. Mr. Drum at Harmonie summed up everything that we had hoped *Drum* could be—fearless, fair, human and critical, with the voice of Africa speaking unmistakably through one of its people. "I did it myself," was an unanswerable argument. "An admirable example of the method of participant observation," said a lecturer in sociology. "Whatever it was, it was hell," said Henry.

But the system of pass laws and contracts, whose abuses we attacked implicitly in Henry's article, was too deeply embedded in South Africa to be changed by a court case, or a visit by a native writer. So long as the system continued, so labourers would continue to be flogged to make them work.

"But these natives are perfectly happy," someone said to me. "You say yourself that they joked and laughed at Harmonie. The natives like to be treated firmly. You don't understand. . . ."

Were we trying to upset some ancient order of Africa, on a quixotic crusade to free people who had no wish for freedom?

But the jokes of Snyman's workers, or the smiling faces of prisoners watching tausa, made the system all the more terrible. They were happy as slaves in the Southern states were happy before their freedom, and afterwards bewildered and wretched.[1] They knew no other life. Their minds had been cast into the mould of slavery.

[1] "Was it any wonder," says Booker Washington in *Up from Slavery*, "that within a few hours the wild rejoicing ceased and a feeling of deep gloom seemed to pervade the slave quarters?"

Farmers and labourers alike had been caught up in the net of contracts, passes, hired convicts, farm prisons, and all the other euphemisms for forced labour. And masters and servants had been degraded and dragged down by the system, which led by easy stages to the death of Elias Mpikwa.

But the savage floggings at Harmonie and Bethal were more than a means to make men work: no man can work when he is dead. The sadistic, insensate beatings had motives deeper than the goading of an ox. They were outbursts of fear and hatred, and a grim omen of what South Africa might become. They showed how men could behave when they held others in absolute power.

*   *   *

We published "I Worked at Snyman's Farm" in *Drum*'s fourth birthday number, in March, 1955, three years after the visit to Bethal. It had by now become a tradition that *Drum*'s birthday numbers should be not gay but grim.

That was the last number of *Drum* that I edited. I had long overstayed the two years' visit that I had planned and, torn like so many others between Africa and Europe, I extricated myself painfully from my fascinating perch. "You English," said Todd; "you either get like the other whites, or else you go home."

Already *Drum* has progressed and changed much since I left, and settled down after its rough and eccentric beginnings; it beats stronger than ever through Africa—south, west and east. The events in this book are only the small and uncertain prelude; but *Drum* had begun to tap the source of African hopes, fears and laughter, and its strength and its faults were those of the Africans themselves; its future is a part of the future of its readers and their troubled continent.

POSTSCRIPT

Africans in Towns

I hope that this book has confused the reader about the character of "the native". It was the main lesson of *Drum* for me and others that Africans were as varied and complicated as any other people. Only the impact of the white man has forced Africans to regard themselves as a single race, and to develop an African nationalism and self-consciousness as a reaction and protection against white domination. The gulf between African intellectuals and labourers, between Arthur and the raw Zulu staring at the upside-down *Drum*, is wider even than in England. Among Africans of one class the difference between, for instance, Can Themba and Todd Matshikiza is at least as great as between an Englishman and a Frenchman.

Africans are sometimes closer to the traditions and culture of Europe than white men misleadingly called "Europeans". The influence of education and environment is far stronger than race. It is a favourite argument for white supremacy that "it has taken us two thousand years to get where we are. How can the natives catch up in fifty years?" But the heritage of Europe is constantly being lost by some and gained by others. The conflict between the civilising influence of Europe and the decadent, savage influence of Africa is not one between races, but between individuals, and within individuals.

Of the nine million Africans in South Africa, two and a half million live in towns, and the number is still increasing rapidly. It is the urban Africans that will play the important role in the future. The old illiterate Africa of blankets and reserves, however picturesque, is insignificant in face of this new industrial proletariat. The urban African is not merely an unhappy displaced person, torn up from his roots: amid the chaos and bewilderment of the shanty towns there is emerging a large settled community, sometimes with three generations of town dwellers behind them. The ancient hierarchy of chiefs and witch doctors in the reserves has been replaced by a new aristocracy of doctors, lawyers, ministers and teachers. There are generations of African children to whom mud huts and tribal rites are as remote as trains are to their country cousins.

In this new Africa of towns and industries, the African has much in common with the European worker in any industrial revolution. The transition of the tribal Zulu from his kraal to Johannesburg, spectacular as it is, is not much more abrupt than that of an English farmhand coming to town a century ago. The South African situation is in some ways only a dramatisation, or a caricature, of the problems of every industrial country, with workers painted black and employers painted white. There is nothing so grim in South Africa today that it cannot be matched by nineteenth-century England: the same tensions and abuses repeat themselves, with the same vicious circle of oppression, protest and more oppression, of violence countered by more violence. But the tensions of colour added to the tensions of class make the conflict more bitter, and the solution more difficult.

South Africa's problem, however much disguised, is fundamentally the problem of different races living together. Sooner or later the question will not be whether whites will tolerate blacks, but whether blacks will tolerate whites. The answer lies in the African locations in the towns.

Most urban Africans are not yet politically minded: they are too preoccupied with finding their own place in the new society, and with the many distractions of city life, to give themselves up to politics. They are still fundamentally conservatives and snobs: the more Europeans classify all natives together, the more educated Africans divorce themselves from "ordinary natives". African leaders are not often in touch with the African masses.

There is as yet no effective African opposition to the government. Congress is at a low ebb: its leaders are nearly all banned or proscribed, and passive resistance has been crushed. The failure to oppose the Sophiatown move or the Bantu Education Act has diminished Congress's reputation. African opposition has stopped short at measures demanding personal sacrifice, and Congress leaders are not prepared to risk five years' imprisonment and lashes for the sake of protest.

When asked to choose between freedom and money, most Africans would still reply "money". To prove it, they trek two thousand miles from the poverty and comparable freedom of Nyasaland to the wealth and restrictions of South Africa.

With an acute shortage of European workers, and a booming economy, industrialists are forced to turn towards Africans for labour, offering more jobs and higher wages. The whole pressure of industry and city life is towards the integration and absorption of Africans into the European way of life and economy, with a blurring of racial differences. The influence of factories, films, shops, books and newspapers is the same on Africans as on Europeans. The more we investigated the reactions of our *Drum* readers, the closer they seemed to European working-class readers.

But as Africans become more absorbed and integrated in the towns, so the government is more determined on its policy of apartheid, which aims to exclude Africans from a permanent place in the white men's cities. While industry pulls Africans towards a European way of life and peaceful integration, apartheid forces him towards nationalism, rejection of European values and leadership, and increasing political self-consciousness.

197

"Thank God for the Nats," said one African Congress leader; "they have united us as nobody else could." By their rejection of all African political advancement, and their use of police powers, the government is now forcing Africans into militant opposition. The defiance campaign would have collapsed in obscurity if it had not been publicised by the display of armed police confronting the "defiers"; and the two thousand police supervising the Sophiatown removal were an undeserved compliment to Congress. The melodramatic raiding of offices, meetings and homes to investigate imaginary "treason and sedition" is more likely to provoke than to cow opposition.

Apartheid will become a boon to extreme African Nationalists, and a menace to the white South Africa which it is designed to preserve. "Our ancestors lost their lives breaking down the old native states," said one United party councillor; "now the government is building them up again, ten miles from here. That's what apartheid means. . . ." The black city south-west of Johannesburg formed by Orlando, Moroka, Jabavu and now Meadowlands, with over two hundred thousand Africans, barred to Europeans, is an easy breeding ground for African nationalism. It is no accident that the most politically active township in South Africa—New Brighton, near Port Elizabeth—is also a model apartheid location, consisting almost entirely of one tribe, Xhosas. "We've got no white friends to prevent us being anti-white: we can be as nationalist as we like," explained a Xhosa leader to me. In the New Brighton riots of 1952, a cinema was gutted and four whites murdered.

I believe Luthuli is correct in saying that extreme nationalism is a greater danger than Communism among Africans. If Communism is not a serious danger, then anti-Communism is. It not only provides a plausible excuse, on the familiar Nazi pattern, for suppressing civil liberties; it also confuses black with red, and by stamping African leaders as Communists intimidates liberal Europeans from supporting them, and so forces Congress to "go it alone".

No African leader at present seriously envisages "Africa for the Africans." In the industrial urban communities of South Africa, the fanatical, retrograde nationalism of the Mau Mau is far distant. But how long can Congress avoid being anti-white in the face of whites so anti-black? Will it be, in the words of Msimangu in *Cry, the Beloved Country* that "when they (the whites) are turned to loving, we will have turned to hating?" The government sincerely believes that Africans will be content within their own strict confines, with their own education, culture, and limited trades. But Africans will only return to their thin roots in a mood of defiance and rejection. The Congress cry of "Come Back Africa" has an ominous ambiguity: it can so easily turn from a cry for freedom and rights, to a cry for a return to a black Africa.

The greatest damage done by apartheid is in the minds of Africans: as whites generalise about "the native", and debit him with all the worst characteristics in themselves, so Africans generalise about "the white man", and associate him with all the unpleasant aspects of authority, discipline, and everything implied by "the baas". The restrictions and humiliations of apartheid are building up a fund of bitterness which will remain long after its cause, as the bitterness of Afrikaners against English reaps its revenge today.

The outlook seems gloomy: it seems difficult to imagine that, with the insults, humiliations and hardships inflicted by apartheid, Africans should not turn to a hard hatred of all white men. Apartheid seems to have been designed to set all blacks against all whites.

But in the shebeens and jive dens of Sophiatown, I could never feel wholly depressed or without hope for the future of South Africa. Bitter though some moments are, Africans have not yet turned to hating: they have a resilience, a gaiety and

199

humour and vitality, and a capacity for suffering and patience, that will not easily turn to despair. There are still friendships across the colour line, and bridges across the gap. The racial clash that the world expects in South Africa is still some way off, and much can happen before then in the world outside to change the tragic course of South Africa.

EPILOGUE

(1983)

When I went back to England in 1955 I thought sadly that I had seen the last of Johannesburg, and that I would lose my links with those remote black townships six thousand miles away. But South Africa soon began to look less remote. Through *Drum* I had met David Astor, the editor of the *Observer*, who was much concerned with black rights in Africa; and he offered me a job as his assistant. The *Observer* kept me in touch with South Africa and soon gave me opportunities for reporting on the continent; while in the mid-fifties apartheid was rapidly attracting more political concern, both in Britain and America, among conservatives as well as liberals and churchmen. When Trevor Huddleston published his book *Naught for Your Comfort* in 1956, describing his experiences in Johannesburg—from which he was soon recalled—he found himself caught up in a wave of political emotion in Britain, with mass meetings and protest marches on behalf of black South Africans. When Chief Luthuli was awarded the Nobel Peace Prize in 1960 he was seen as a hero by both the Left and the Right in Europe.

In London I was sporadically involved in the anti-apartheid protests, and sometimes found myself awkwardly sitting on platforms alongside missionaries, Labour politicians or South African Communist exiles. After the glaring simplicities of the issues in Johannesburg I felt bewildered by the hostility between the anti-apartheid factions in London—the Communists and anti-Communists, the moderates and extremists, the Christians and agnostics. I was amused to find myself, the ex-editor of a

201

pop magazine which had flourished on pin-ups and crime stories, taking part in high-minded meetings about race relations and Church responsibilities. I was quite relieved that few of my new friends had actually seen a copy of the magazine with its smudgy photographs and strident headlines on yellowing newsprint. But I reassured myself that I probably knew more than most of them about the daily lives and the real aspirations of the victims of apartheid. It was a time when Western liberals were apt to attribute every virtue to suffering blacks and to entertain impossible hopes for the emerging independent states, and there was no harm in reminding them that black South Africa had its full share of gangsters, drunks and human failings.

I found the slow-moving British political institutions and the impersonal committees an abrupt anti-climax after the open conflicts and individual challenges in South Africa, where the ruthless workings of power and the courage of rebels was so much more obvious; and it took me a long time to feel myself involved in the British system. For years I felt myself a kind of exile even though I had spent only four years in South Africa, and I seized every excuse to return. I went back to Johannesburg to write a book on the Treason Trial in 1957, when many black friends had been arrested and charged with conspiring against the state; I flew out to Rhodesia and Nyasaland (Zimbabwe and Malawi) to report successive crises for the *Observer*, always making detours to Johannesburg. British politicians were becoming more concerned with the African continent, and with the tensions inside South Africa, as the process of decolonising was gathering pace. The worlds of London and Johannesburg were looking less impossibly distant. 1960 was proclaimed as the climactic "Year of Decision" for Africa, and early in that year I followed the British Prime Minister Harold Macmillan on his tour of the continent, writing the "Pendennis" column in the *Observer*. I kept on badgering Macmillan's staff about the dangers of appeasing white South Africa, and my friend Tim Bligh, who was Macmillan's principal private secretary, kept assuring me that the draft of the final speech to be made in Cape Town included a denunciation of apartheid. As Macmillan made his way cautiously through Ghana, Nigeria and Rhodesia, Tim promised me: "It's still in; it's still in." Then in Cape Town I listened in astonishment from the press gallery of the Parliament to Macmillan delivering his historic "Wind of Change" speech in which he politely but very firmly disassociated the British government from the policies of Dr. Verwoerd.

A few months later, the force of that wind was suddenly more evident: the Congo was granted independence and was immediately rent by civil war, while in South Africa the police killed sixty black demonstrators in Sharpeville, causing a wave of protests and arrests all over the country. I was back in Johannesburg during that crisis; blacks defied the police and made bonfires of their hated pass-books; Dr. Verwoerd was shot by a mad white farmer and for a few days the pressure of black anger and world opinion seemed to be bending the rigid structure of white supremacy. But it was a false dawn. The police counter-attacked, Verwoerd recovered, the laws were tightened, and the secret service was thoroughly retrained with the help of Britain and France. The battle-lines between black and white were drawn more firmly than ever, and the Pretoria government became more intransigent and isolated than ever. A year later black member states led by Nigeria forced South Africa to leave the British Commonwealth.

White liberals who hoped to see a gradual movement on the American pattern towards a multi-racial South Africa were now caught between black and white nationalisms. Some, like Harry Oppenheimer of the Anglo-American Corporation, still put their hopes on the fast-growing prosperity which, they believed, would create a skilled black labour force and eventually alleviate the race conflicts; a few tried to join forces with the black nationalists, to launch their own terrorist movements, or to campaign for boycotts; but more and more emigrated to Britain, America or Australia, in the belief that their own country was heading for a bloodbath. For myself I could see no role, and no hopeful outcome. I observed a new milestone in 1964, when as a reporter for the *Observer* I watched the trial in Pretoria of Nelson Mandela and other leaders accused of plotting against the state. Mandela asked me, through his lawyer Bram Fisher, to help draft his speech to the court—the opportunity for a political statement which the judge could not deny him. A few weeks later he delivered his long unrepentant last speech and was sentenced to life imprisonment on Robben Island, off the coast of the Cape. With the disappearance of Mandela, the wisest and most representative of the black leaders, the prospects of any eventual compromise in South Africa seemed much more remote. The black South Africans put their remaining hopes in pressures from outside—from the United Nations, from Western or Eastern capitals, and increasingly from guerrilla fighters.

I was now writing mostly about Britain but I still saw South Africa as a touchstone and yardstick for my political values, and the source of most of my political education: the predicaments of the poor in early nineteenth-century Britain and America seemed much more imaginable from the slums of Soweto. Africa had been my university, more than Oxford; and most of my real friendships, white as well as black, dated from that African experience. When I was writing my first long political book, *Anatomy of Britain*, in 1962 I could more easily empathise with politicians—from Iain Macleod to Shirley Williams—who were emotionally involved in African issues. Two days before *Anatomy* was published I fled the country, leaving my long-suffering publishers to promote the book—to Johannesburg. As I stepped on to the South African plane in Rome, the Calvinist faces and jarring accents of the Afrikaner air hostesses suddenly brought back all the old associations of bigotry, joylessness and oppression, and I wondered why on earth I should be spending part of my bonanza on going there, rather than to New York, Rome or Paris. But once I was back in Johannesburg and Soweto I remembered why: that these turbulent cities still generated the kind of vitality and immediacy which I could never find in the labyrinths of Whitehall and Westminster. It was a sort of going home.

I often felt torn between the heady world of power in London—to which journalists have such easy but illusory access—and the much more personal and emotional world of Johannesburg, where the issues seemed so much more real and individual. The dichotomy was brought home to me one day when a Scots minister had asked to meet me in London: "What I've really come to ask you about," he explained, "is this: how can you reconcile your radical interest in Africa with your baroque interest in power?" The question bothered me, as it was meant to, and I was only partially reassured when I realised that my questioner too was ambivalent; and that many radical politicians shared the dichotomy.

Certainly the moral issues of Africa were becoming much less clear-cut; and the tyrannies and convulsions of many new black states to the north made any future for South Africa look less hopeful. Like others I often felt exasperated by a sense of the perversity of Africa—the preposterous black rhetoric, the second-rate standards, the insistence on playing out the worst elements of nationalism with coups, massacres and civil wars. The white communities in Rhodesia and South Africa seemed equally determined to go to hell in their own stubborn way, cultivating their own myths and complacencies until they finally cut the lifelines that held them to Europe. The West began to lose interest in a continent which refused to conform to the image prepared for it. But South Africa would not go away: it remained inescapably a Western problem whose consequences were reverberating still more loudly in London and Washington. It was the most dangerous frontier of Western enterprise, diplomacy and defence; and the test-bed for Western attitudes to race. Whenever I returned to Johannesburg it still seemed like a crude stage lit by arc-lights which lit up with long shadows the behaviour of people when faced with great power or power-lessness. Compared to the committees and delegations of Britain and its entrenched institutions, South Africa still seemed a country of individual heroes or villains who were facing real issues and challenges.

II

As for *Drum*, the end of my book marked only one phase of its erratic and variegated story—which others have taken up—as it was caught up in the storms of independent Africa. I kept in touch with successive editors and writers in different parts of the continent, and though I was now only a spectator *Drum* remained an open-sesame to odd corners of African life. My first successor as editor in Johannesburg, Sylvester Stein, was a South African journalist from the *Rand Daily Mail* who gave the magazine his own stamp; he was a keen athlete (he later became a founder of the veteran Olympics who held their own world championships) and one of his first *Drum* features revealed that Olympic teams could be disqualified if they had been selected according to race—an exposure which helped to activate the momentous anti-apartheid movement in sport. "Mr. Drum" continued his investigations, most notably when Can Themba tried to join the congregations of white Johannesburg churches of different denominations, with Jurgen Schadeberg as photographer recording the scene, to see how he would be welcomed: when he went to the Seventh Day Adventists the congregation chased him and Schadeberg out of the church in their fury.

Soon afterwards Dr. Verwoerd's government tried to pass a bill to enforce strict racial divisions in Christian churches—which the Anglican Church effectively prevented, by insisting that its cathedrals and churches were open to all. Stein's career with the *Drum* organisation finished abruptly. He had chosen for the cover a photograph of the black tennis-player Althea Gibson kissing a white player in America; Jim Bailey refused to allow the cover in South Africa, regarding it as a needless provocation of the government, and Stein resigned and soon afterwards went to London, where he wrote novels and established his own business in trade magazines.

Stein was followed by Tom Hopkinson, the celebrated former editor of the British magazine *Picture Post*. He already knew a good deal about *Drum* since its early days when Jim had asked him to give advice from London, since neither Jim nor I knew anything about magazine layout. I used to airmail him copies of the magazine and he sent back neat little commentaries with diagrams, complaining about the "radish-shaped horrors" of pages ruined by advertising and showing how it should be done—an invaluable correspondence course. He had become sufficiently interested in *Drum* and its opportunities to accept Jim's invitation to come out to Africa as its editor-in-chief, at the age of fifty-three. He brought with him his own fastidious standards as a journalist; he produced a much more professional and disciplined magazine with more sensitive use of picture-journalism: "Now the photographs are going to *be* the paper," he told his staff.[1] He encouraged and trained several young photographers including Peter Magubene and Ian Berry who achieved world reputations.

Tom looked over the chaotic *Drum* office from his glass-panelled sanctum with his huge soulful eyes—"the penetrating, round, bulging and sorrowful eyes of an owl"—as his Nigeria editor Nelson Ottah described them. He had his own vision of

[1] Tom Hopkinson: *In The Fiery Continent*, Gollancz, London, 1962, p.27.

207

a future all-African multi-racial *Drum* and he was excited by the original and creative black writers, but he was more distressed than I was by their lack of professional training: "What terrific journalists they would make with only a few months' training." He left, after his own disagreements with Jim Bailey who wanted to double the price of the magazine, and later set up his own centre to train black journalists in Nairobi. "The three and a half years with *Drum*," he wrote later, "have profoundly affected my whole life."[1]

After Tom Hopkinson's departure the task of editing *Drum* in South Africa became increasingly difficult, as legislation and censorship prevented any candid reporting of politics. "Named" politicians or writers could not even be mentioned in print; any reporting of discontent could be prosecuted as incitement; any subversive literature had to be reported to the police; and there were recurring suspicions about police informers on the staff. Successive white editors grappled as they could to produce a magazine which represented the black readers' interests, including sport, jazz, pin-ups, crime and events in the rest of Africa. But *Drum* was always walking a tight-rope between its readers and the police; and the absence of politics left a huge gap.

It was the black writers and photographers who provided the real character and continuity of *Drum*, and who bore the greatest strains and risks of the job; the casualty rate was appalling, whether from drink, politics or from township gangsters. Henry Nxumalo, the bravest and most original of the magazine's investigative journalists (in the real sense of the term), who had exposed Bethal, the jail conditions and the murderous farm at Harmonie, was found one day stabbed to death in a gutter in Soweto; no one could ever prove who had murdered him or why, though his colleagues suspected that it was a racketeer

[1] *The Beat of Drum*: anthology published by *Drum* and the Ravan Press, Johannesburg, 1982, pp.110, 124.

whom Henry had been investigating. Todd Matshikiza, who had been *Drum*'s jazz critic, became more famous as the composer of the black jazz musical *King Kong* which after a spectacular success in Johannesburg was shown with its original black cast in London. Todd himself lived for a time in London, about which he wrote a book, *Chocolates for My Wife*,[1] but he never felt really at home in Britain, or in Zambia where he moved; he was drinking heavily and died tragically early. (His son John is now a successful actor in Britain, and his widow Esme later married the Namibian political leader Andreas Shipanga.) Can Themba continued at his best to write brilliantly, with his own sparkling use of English. ("Africans are creating out of English a language of their own," he wrote in one anthology: "language that thinks in actions, using words that dart back and forth on quick-moving fact, virile, earthy, garrulous."[2]) But he became increasingly erratic and hard-drinking as assistant editor of *Drum*: Tom Hopkinson eventually felt compelled to fire him and he retreated to Swaziland to teach at a mission school on a mountain-top; but he could never forswear alcohol and he died of a heart attack while reading a newspaper in bed. Bob Gosani, Henry Nxumalo's nephew, continued sporadically to take superb photographs, interspersed with heavy drinking bouts which eventually took him, too, to an early death.

The record of disasters continued: Casey Motsisi, the protégé of Can Themba and Tom Hopkinson who became a racy columnist in Damon Runyon style,[3] also succumbed to drink. Nat Nakasa, a gifted young Zulu writer, went to live in New York where he could never feel himself at home; but he was refused a passport to return home and he committed suicide

---

[1] Hodder and Stoughton, 1961.
[2] Introduction to *Darkness and Light* (edited by Peggy Rutherfoord), Faith Press, 1958.
[3] See Casey & Co: *Selected Writings of Casey "Kid" Motsisi*, Johannesburg, Ravan Press, 1978.

from the top of a skyscraper. One of the most remarkable *Drum* graduates was David Sibeko, a huge young African from Soweto whom I hired to work the *Drum* telephone exchange. He was unflappable, not intellectual and always genial, but the horrors of Sharpeville impelled him into politics, and he was soon accused—with some formidable evidence—of trying to assassinate Dr. Verwoerd. He was acquitted with the help of an able lawyer and a fund raised by old friends and went on to become a leader of the Pan African Congress, and their Ambassador Plenipotentiary in London and New York. He often visited me in London on the way between Peking, the U.N. and Africa, recounting extraordinary adventures with deep laughter. Then in 1979 he was murdered by unknown assassins hired by political rivals in Dar es Salaam.

The strains for any courageous and honest journalist in the worsening climate of South Africa were increasingly impossible, but there were some magnificent survivors. Peter Magubane, who joined *Drum* as a van-driver and was trained by Jurgen Schadeberg and Tom Hopkinson to become a world-class photographer, continued to move in and out of South Africa, taking superb pictures which have been much exhibited in America and Europe.[1] Ezekiel Mphahlele, the scholarly teacher who became *Drum*'s literary editor, became a professor in Nairobi, Zambia, Denver and Philadelphia before he insisted on returning to teach in South Africa. Others prospered in exile, trying to put South Africa behind them. Arthur Maimane, who had joined *Drum* as a versatile cub reporter in its first months, became a successful journalist in London, where he now works on Independent Television News. Bloke Modisane, the short-story writer from Sophiatown, escaped through Central Africa, wrote and acted in Britain and America, and published his own memoir *Blame Me on History*.[2] Lewis Nkosi,

[1] See for instance *Magubane's South Africa*, Secker & Warburg, London, 1978.
[2] Thames & Hudson, London, 1963.

the Zulu writer and critic, worked and studied in London and New York before returning to Africa to teach at the University of Zambia in Lusaka. Andy Anderson, the Falstaffian Coloured printer who entertained journalists and politicians in his Johannesburg printing shop, later settled in Lesotho with a thriving dry-cleaning business and his hospitality intact. The enterprise and creativity of many of these black South Africans could survive successive blows to their freedom and security: their combination of sensitivity, humour and resilience, of education and harsh experience—like that of earlier Jewish refugees—contributed much to other communities. The loss to South Africa of this kind of creative and imaginative spirit was more visible each time I returned to Johannesburg, as the constraints of political freedom inhibited freedom of expression in all the arts.

III

At the beginning of the sixties, in the wake of the Sharpeville massacre, the governments of Dr. Verwoerd and John Vorster were pushing through new laws to crush any black opposition, to remove freedoms and to censor the press. When they forbade newspapers to mention the names of proscribed black politicians or the activities of their organisations, they made political reporting absurd and narrowly circumscribed the scope of *Drum* (and even more of the *Golden City Post*, the Sunday paper which Jim Bailey and Cecil Eprile had started just after I left). "It was dull work," Tom Hopkinson later wrote, "editing a magazine in which almost nothing could be said."[1] After Hopkinson left, subsequent *Drum* editors in South Africa had to content

[1] *In the Fiery Continent*, p.293.

211

themselves largely with sport, jazz, pin-ups and human interest stories about the black townships.

But in the meantime *Drum* was beating through other parts of the continent. Already in its first years Jim and I had dreams about a kind of *Life* of Africa, which would help to bring a common awareness to the black territories which were feeling their way towards independence. Our first attempts to spread *Drum* northwards were full of comic cross-purposes and fiascoes: I used to go up to Salisbury and Bulawayo to try to sell copies in the townships, but the black Rhodesians in the fifties seemed politically and intellectually a generation behind the black South Africans and showed little interest in their brothers south of the Zambezi. A more promising English-speaking area was West Africa, where Jim Bailey had invited another young Englishman, Anthony Smith—who had worked on the *Guardian* after writing his first book, *Blind White Fish in Persia*—to set up an office, which he did with intrepid adventures, helped by his local manager Willie Cooke in Ghana and Dapo Fatogun in Nigeria. But communications between the Gold Coast and Johannesburg were primitive: a slow boat sailed unpredictably every few weeks from Cape Town to Accra, later supplemented by a Pan-Am plane once a week. Anthony complained patiently about packets of *Drum* arriving six months late, riddled with worms; they were, he complained, "thick with stories of un-believable irrelevance to our West African lives: profiles of unknown heroes, accounts of gangsters, love stories whose names, places and details were quite alien." But gradually communications improved, special West African pages were included and *Drum* began to be seen as an authentic black magazine in the Gold Coast and Nigeria.

The Gold Coast, which as Ghana was to be the first British African colony to achieve independence, exerted a special fascination over the world in the late fifties, with its exuberant rhetoric and limitless ambitions: the charisma of its first Prime

Minister or "Redeemer", Kwame Nkrumah, cast a spell over whites as well as blacks, luring bankers, idealists, statesmen and international cranks to its optimistic shores. But it was not long before Ghana was putting up the same kind of obstacles to a free press that *Drum* was already experiencing in South Africa. In the early years under Anthony Smith and his Ghanaian successor, Cameron Duodu, *Drum* was able to maintain its independence from Nkrumah's propaganda machine; but since the West African *Drum* was printed in Johannesburg it was always open to the charge of South African influence. By 1960 the Ghana government were exasperated by *Drum*'s publicising of the leader of the opposition, J. B. Danquah: by a bitter irony it was the police shooting at Sharpeville, which *Drum* had helped to display round the world, that gave Nkrumah the excuse to ban *Drum* as a South African product, and it was only with exhaustive lobbying and messages of support from allies like Trevor Huddleston and Basil Davidson that Jim Bailey could get the ban lifted. *Drum*'s career in Ghana continued to be very uncertain as Ghana's economic prospects declined while Nkrumah's paranoia increased (I had my own brief glimpse of it, when I was visiting Ghana for the *Observer* and found myself spending a night in one of Nkrumah's jails). After Nkrumah was deposed in 1966, followed by successive coups and counter-coups, *Drum* faced growing difficulties in a bankrupt nation run by corrupt rulers, until after twenty years' effort Jim Bailey finally had to liquidate the company and "wait for honest times".

It was Nigeria, with far the biggest population in Africa, which gave *Drum* the greatest opportunity of all, much boosted by a brilliant young Ibo editor, Nelson Ottah, who wrote with a political extraversion very different from the black South Africans. Ottah rode high on the independence of Nigeria: he achieved his first great coup with a series on the early life of the Nigerian publisher-politician Dr. Azikiwe, and he later worked closely with Tom Hopkinson as his editor-in-chief, and with Alun Morris, the young "Welsh wizard" who took over Hopkinson's role in 1960 and threw himself into Nigerian life. But in 1966, just after the ruler of Northern Nigeria, the Sardauna of Sokoto, had been assassinated, Ottah published a rash obituary attacking the dead ruler, which enraged the Northerners who suspected the Ibos of having executed a coup; and Ottah had to go into hiding to escape with his life: "One maladroit step," as he put it, "not conceived or taken by me, had reduced me from an arrogant editor of a successful magazine to a frightened rabbit scurrying from one hiding place to another." Drum's problems in Nigeria were soon compounded by the civil war, in which Ottah later took charge of Biafran propaganda. After the war Ottah returned briefly to Drum, but without the same zest, and before long the magazine was threatened by a new decree which forbade foreign ownership of Nigerian media; both Jim Bailey and Nelson Ottah were found to be unacceptable, and the magazine had to be sold to Nigerian owners. Ottah still looked back with warmth on his experience: "On the whole, Drum was not a dream without fulfilment," he wrote afterwards,

> or a hope turned into a mirage, or a magic maimed by incongruity. Nor was Drum all black and white. It was grey. It was not all simple. It was grand—as grand as the great dream of the both simple and complicated patrician who conceived it and gave it everything, in his simple and yet complicated way, that he thought and believed would make it boom.[1]

In the late fifties and sixties Drum was expanding all over black Africa, caught up in all the turmoils of colonial wars and newly independent states. After I had left Johannesburg Jim

[1] The Beat of Drum, p.120.

Bailey looked more seriously to East Africa where the three linked British colonies—Kenya, Uganda and Tanganyika—were beginning to demand independence, culminating in the Mau Mau revolt. To set up *Drum* in Nairobi Jim invited yet another young Oxford graduate, Alan Rake, whom I had introduced to Jim, to come out to Africa. I had met him when he had invited me to talk to the Oxford University Press Club about the magazine. It was (as Alan later described it) "the very stuff to fire a young man's imagination. . . . I knew it was where I wanted to be." In Nairobi Alan soon decided that there was no point in "slavishly copying the formula that had built *Drum* in South Africa. Sex, crime and campaigns against social injustice were all good standbys, but what the African readership in Kenya wanted was a magazine which identified itself with the African political struggle for independence."[1]

Rake and *Drum* were soon in the midst of East African upheavals. In Tanganyika (later Tanzania) both Rake and Bailey were close to Julius Nyerere, the founder–president of the new nation. In Kenya Rake was embroiled in the internal conflicts after the ending of the Mau Mau rebellion. *Drum* published the first evidence that Jomo Kenyatta—then still detained in prison—had been convicted on perjured testimony (a view that was later reinforced by evidence that the judge had himself been bribed by the Governor-General, Sir Evelyn Baring). Rake became a close friend of Tom Mboya, the young black trade unionist whom President Kenyatta appointed as Minister of Finance, and was writing his biography when he was mysteriously assassinated in 1969. Rake built up a remarkable team and following, until Jim Bailey decided that he could not finance a separate edition in East Africa, when Rake took charge of *Drum*'s West African offices.

In Uganda, which was already suffering tragic convulsions before independence, *Drum* was one of the first organs to take

[1] *The Beat of Drum*, p.56.

seriously the career of Milton Obote, who became President until he was ousted by Idi Amin. When Amin began his reign of terror against Obote's followers and tribesmen, *Drum* was one of the first to expose its full horrors and to show that the main sufferers were not the few foreigners but the tens of thousands of black prisoners in Uganda. When other African states were insisting on respecting Amin's autonomy, *Drum* published an outspoken editorial insisting that the rest of Africa could no longer hold off. Not long afterwards, the Tanzanian army moved into Uganda, for the thankless task of removing Amin.

IV

Through all its ups and downs, its expansions and contractions, the connecting thread of *Drum* was not so much the continent or the "African personality" as the personality of its owner Jim Bailey, who flew endlessly between its scattered components trying to hold them together. He was always more interested in journalism than in money; and his own journalistic flair often raced ahead of his editors'. As his managerial problems became more burdensome he still cultivated his own bohemian lifestyle, breezing in and out of London or New York in sports coat, snakeskin tie and dirty shoes, and drifting off from his meetings with lawyers and accountants to enjoy an evening's drinking and story-telling with eccentric cronies. He remained intensely curious about the more macabre aspects of Africa—particularly about the lingering traditions of human sacrifice and ritual murders, about which he developed his own theories—and built up his own unique range of sources about all aspects of Africa from presidents and governors-general to witch doctors and shebeen-keepers. He could move happily from black Johannesburg slums to the ancient rituals of tribal Africa; when he wanted to improve *Drum*'s relations in Northern Nigeria he organised an English polo team to come out to play a team organised by the Emir of Katsina. In his fascination with magic and ju-ju Jim had certainly imbibed old Africa; but he was taken aback by the galloping ambition for materialism and money: "Mammon became the great god of Africa," he lamented—"so much so that I was led almost to believe that the principal drive behind the illustrious liberatory movements had rarely been freedom but had always been cash."[1]

As Jim's empire expanded he was much more occupied with finance, with printing presses and with overseeing management; and he often wished he could be more of an editor, less of a manager. His overriding duty, as he saw it, was to keep his magazines intact, and he resented editors who invited clashes with governments—"the editor wears the halo, everybody else goes to the stake." But he still sparked off editorial ideas wherever he went. "He was a master of general ideas," as Ottah put it,

> although all his ideas, as I came to examine them more closely, tended to be quaint. He threw these ideas about, whether in conferences with his editors or while, to use his pet expression, he was 'splitting' a bottle of beer (which he invariably made sure not to pay for) with them. He, in my days, hated being pinned down—down to the practicalities of his overflowing ideas.[2]

His personality continued to baffle successive editors and staff. He liked to show his commercial toughness in the tradition of his formidable father, the gold tycoon Sir Abe Bailey; he also loved to defy the rich white Johannesburg world around him,

[1] *The Beat of Drum*, p.155.
[2] Ibid, p.101.

and he hung on to *Drum* through all its troubles. He was, as
Tom Hopkinson said,

> the one constant thread throughout its history. Only someone
> with a strong streak of idealism in his nature would have used
> a personal fortune in this way; and only someone with a great
> deal of practical understanding could have managed to keep
> the magazine from foundering many times over on the reefs of
> national hostility, and of racial and personal antagonisms.[1]

He saw *Drum*'s responsibility in Africa as being "to take part
in disseminating ideas; to continue to maintain a pan-African
link and use a quiet, discriminating faculty. . . . to encourage
and train authors, photographers and illustrators as well as
businessmen; and act as a social yeast or catalyst."[2] He was
sometimes moved to use his influence directly to try to change
events. Before the East African colonies became independent
he was convinced by Tom Mboya and Julius Nyerere that they
should maintain a federation which could reinforce their
economies, and he lobbied the Conservative minister Lord
Alport, though without results. After the independence of
Nigeria, when the federation was disintegrating and the
Northern leader, the Sardauna of Sokoto, had been assassinated,
Jim tried to lobby the British Prime Minister Harold Wilson to
summon a constitutional conference to avert civil war in Nigeria;
but likewise without success.

At its peak Jim was able to survey a unique magazine empire.
"The *Drum* organisation in the 1960s," he recollected,

> covered English-speaking Africa from the borders of Ethiopia
> to Cape Town: from Sierra Leone and Liberia to Windhoek.
> It was a great popular educator. It was a huge communication

[1] *The Beat of Drum*, p.21.
[2] Ibid, p.140.

structure across our African continent, with a tiny stem in the person of myself. It would not have been difficult to have obtained outside money that had political strings attached: indeed, like others, I could have extracted a fortune from such subsidies. But since integrity was what we were really selling, this was hardly acceptable. One blow after another then began to destroy my organisation.

Organisation was perhaps too strong a word, for *Drum* was always built round Jim's personality, and it was hard to find the kind of stable managerial partner to complement his own flair. To control and co-ordinate magazines across the African divides needed unusual management skills, and Jim's restless travels, arriving and departing unpredictably with a set of new projects and ideas, increased the needs. He hated to be pinned down and dreaded losing his own autonomy by sharing control with a co-owner or strong chief executive. He did find some remarkable managers but his casual approach to hiring on instinct—for which many of his journalists were grateful—led to some high risks.

But the real threat to *Drum* lay in the constraints of Africa. As South Africa and the new black states all became more intolerant, the future of an independent magazine which crossed over their frontiers became much more perilous. The pages of *Drum* tried to give their own chronicle of the horrors of intolerance, with photographs of mass executions, beatings and police raids. But the hopes that *Drum* could maintain its freedom in the new black states soon faded: "Governments and leaders felt themselves too insecure to allow criticism of any kind," as Tom Hopkinson said, "and without some degree of independence for himself no journalist or editor can function and no newspaper or magazine they may produce will be worth reading." "Don't talk to me about 'freedom of the press'!" Tom Mboya told Hopkinson in Kenya: "No such thing exists! When the white man ruled Kenya the newspapers all supported the white governments—they told me that was their duty. Well, now we're the government!"[1]

With the growing clamour for "Africanisation" the fact that *Drum* was owned by a white South African gave an easy excuse for black governments to complain about any critical articles. When *Drum* was expropriated in Nigeria, the biggest African market of all, the hopes of a Pan-African magazine receded further. The black nations were becoming more engrossed in their own pressing problems, economic crises, and disputes with their neighbours; the concepts of African unity and the African Personality which Nkrumah had heralded in Ghana became increasingly hazy. The different *Drum*s still shared some common characteristics and attitudes, and some common heroes, like black Olympic sportsmen and film stars. But the dream of the great Pan-African *Drum*, to be like *Life* in America in the forties, faded with the surge of African nationalism.

In South Africa itself *Drum* faced its toughest problems. Jim still spent most of his time there, on his farm outside Johannesburg with a growing family round him, involving himself with farming and Bronze-Age history as well as the magazine. As the apartheid laws added new constraints Jim insisted that the magazine's first duty was to survive, and not risk total confrontation with a merciless government. The scope for political coverage and social exposure narrowed still further. Even when treading the most cautious political path *Drum* was surrounded by commercial as well as political enemies, and its sister-paper, the weekly *Golden City Post*, was specially vulnerable. In 1967 Jim had found himself over-committed to an expensive gravure magazine press in Johannesburg. The Argus newspaper group—controlling most English-speaking papers in South Africa, and owned by the giant Anglo-American corporation—took the opportunity to undercut the *Post* with

[1] *The Beat of Drum*, p.24.

their own black newspaper, and eventually Jim was forced to sell the *Post* to them (which not long afterwards was banned by the government). For Jim it was a bitter moment to have to sell the newspaper he had launched twelve years earlier to the Anglo-American monopoly:

> when, as I struggled on the surface, the sharks rose up out of the deep to snatch their mouthful out of the one who was in difficulties, and the various parasites crept from the wainscoting of my debts, so that my world suddenly became peopled with nightmare creatures, it was natural to hark back nostalgically to the days of the beginnings—to the chair, to the table and the one wastepaper basket, when we purchased our first typewriter with the sentiment of affluence and when chance visitors looked in off the street. We balanced our trading accounts with a few pounds either way and the important thing in life—friends—predominated.[1]

Drum itself survived the crash of its sister *Post*; but as an organ of black opinion, however muffled, it remained an object of suspicion to the South African government. So it was hardly surprising that when B.O.S.S., the secret police organisation in Pretoria, with the help of the Director of Information Dr. Rhoodie, planned their great conspiracy in the mid-seventies to control the English-speaking press, *Drum* was one of their prime targets. Rhoodie had already tried—and only just failed—to buy control of the *Rand Daily Mail* in Johannesburg, under cover provided by an Afrikaner fertiliser tycoon; and he had launched the weekly *Citizen* and the magazine *To the Point* under concealed government ownership. He had secretly financed the American newspaper-owner John McGoff who propagated the case for apartheid in his papers, and he even had his own director on the board of Independent Television News

[1] *The Beat of Drum*, p.128.

in London. He was inevitably tempted to buy *Drum* as a mouthpiece to influence black opinion. Before the secret plot in Pretoria had been revealed, Jim Bailey was approached via the South African financier David Abramson by the British publisher Christopher Dolley—the former chairman of Penguin books—to sell the whole *Drum* magazine group. Jim was now approaching sixty and "resented the amount of time, of sheer brain-power that my beloved publishing mistress exacted from me". He was tempted to offload his heavy financial commitment in return for £363,000 but he was suspicious of Dolley, and played for time: Dolley tried to claim that the deal had already been agreed, and threatened to start a rival magazine with limitless cash. Jim still refused, and the rival magazine, called *Pace*, went ahead. But soon the whole secret Pretoria conspiracy to capture the media—with Abramson and Dolley in the midst of it—was revealed by a succession of exposures in Johannesburg papers; and the first issue of *Pace* coincided with the full international exposure of the scandal, which *Drum* reported with relish. Not long afterwards *Pace* was put up for sale.

V

Drum, though its all-African heyday was over, could still keep going in South Africa, in East Africa and in Zimbabwe; and in 1981 it celebrated its thirtieth anniversary with an anthology, *The Beat of Drum*, which looked back with photographs and reminiscences on the vicissitudes of the continent and the magazine. "Thirty years of publishing," Jim wrote, "has shown me that when our publics had the facts they were able to make healthy and sane judgments for themselves. Dictatorship was always preceded by muzzling of the press."[1]

[1] *The Beat of Drum*, p.168.

Looking back on my own experience thirty years earlier, and on the yellowing and disintegrating pages of the first issues of *Drum*, I had to admit that their picture of black South Africa had been too light-hearted and too optimistic, and that we had underestimated the extent of the tyranny and hardships that would follow. I wished I had taken more advantage of my access to the townships to investigate more seriously the roots of black politics. From the perspective of the years after Sharpeville, the passive resistance, the multi-racial ambitions and the skirmishes with the police in the early fifties looked like a false dawn of liberalism before the gates of apartheid closed more firmly, and the police and secret services mobilised themselves more systematically to stamp out political protest. The courageous hopes of people such as Henry Nxumalo and Todd Matshikiza seemed like the last bridges between the black and white worlds: each time I returned to Johannesburg in the sixties and seventies the divide seemed wider, the bridges fewer. The new black political generation did not believe that passive resistance and non-violence could ever give them their freedom, or that they could trust white supporters, and they wisely kept themselves to themselves: any visitor to Soweto risked getting his black host into trouble more than himself. By the mid-sixties most of my own black friends were in exile, or in prison, or dead. In the embattled and polarised political atmosphere few out-siders—and certainly not the police—were able to detect the real groundswells and undercurrents of black politics. When riots broke out in Soweto in 1976, followed by unprecedented police reprisals and a new wave of international disgust, no journalist could claim to have predicted them.

The black South Africans in the townships, I believe, will still hold the key to the peace and prosperity of their country; and the future balance of forces in Africa will depend on the political attitudes of the few million blacks in the Southern industrial centres. The Western nations—particularly the

United States—still frequently misunderstand their political motivations, and equate their nationalism with Communism because they have sought help from Moscow or Peking. But the black leaders continue to see their liberation from white domination as the overriding issue, and to judge other countries as friends or enemies according to their stand on apartheid. When I returned to Johannesburg in November, 1978, at the time of the Muldergate scandal and the elections in Namibia, I went back to Soweto, past the still-visible wreckage of the riots, to see Dr. Nthato Motlana—one of the few political survivors—whom I had first known as a political young doctor thirty years ago. "Why do you people in Britain and America still keep on supporting apartheid with your investments and banks?" he asked me. "You're giving my people no alternative—they have to look for friends in the East."

This book I hope offers some evidence of the extent to which black South Africans have looked to the West for their friendships, common culture and Christianity. The black writers on *Drum*, most of them educated in mission schools in a language enriched by the Bible and Shakespeare, were more Westernised in many ways than most Afrikaners. (The British—whether in India, Africa or the West Indies—have often enough seen how their own culture and language can be revived and refreshed by the foreign peoples to whom they had taught it.) But Western appeasers, who allow the gates of apartheid to close against Western culture, betray the tradition of their own civilisation. If they are thus isolated, black South Africans will inevitably look to the Communist states which have always seen South Africa as a textbook case for a Marxist revolution. They will become gradually Easternised as once they were Westernised. But as they do so, the West will have themselves to blame.